COACHWORK ON VINTAGE
BENTLEYS

COACHWORK ON VINTAGE
BENTLEYS

BY NICK WALKER

Herridge & Sons

Published in 2005 by
Herridge & Sons Ltd
Lower Forda, Shebbear,
Beaworthy, Devon EX21 5SY

Reprinted 2021

Designed by Jonathan Davison
Special photography by Rowan Isaac

ISBN 978-0-9549981-1-0
Printed in China

Picture Acknowledgments
The author and the publisher are grateful to the following, who have contributed photographs reproduced in this book:
Tim Houlding, Bryan Goodman, Paul Harrison, Chris Storrar, Neill Bruce, David Hodges Collection

Contents

Introduction and Acknowledgments

When Walter Owen Bentley set out after the First World War to design his own car, he can hardly have realised what a tumultuous few years lay before him. All he wanted was to produce high-quality, sporting cars which would appeal to affluent buyers looking for good performance. He could hardly have expected that, during the ten short years that his cars were on the market, they would become the most famous, most sought-after British marque of the period – indeed, probably of all time. Even less did he expect that this fame would attract owners who would probably never use the car's fabulous performance, and who would be content to use their fine new possession as no more than a town carriage.

It is this contrast between the image of the vintage

One of the oldest Bentleys in existence, chassis 19, this two-seater Three Litre from the end of 1921 bears coachwork by the Edinburgh firm of Gairn.

Bentley and the reality which is one of the many fascinating aspects of its history. Most of us know, in more or less detail, the story of their five wins at Le Mans (four of them in a row), and most of us are familiar with the sight of these cars today – almost all in the form of a tourer or some other sporting coachwork. Yet how many of us are aware that the majority of these cars were delivered with rather more mundane body styles? This is not to denigrate the excellent coachbuilders who produced all those saloons, limousines, landaulets, cabriolets and drop-head coupés which formed the major portion of Bentley bodies sold, nor in many cases the buyers who ordered them. There is nothing to be criticised in an owner requiring a closed car for his family or his business, and yet desiring the maximum performance from his car.

On the other hand there seem to have been numerous buyers who were indifferent to the effect of increased weight on performance, and who insisted on closed bodies of the greatest luxury, and consequently of considerable weight. Worse, they demanded more interior space – particularly legroom – than the standard chassis could provide, with the result that Bentley was obliged to produce chassis with longer and longer wheelbase dimensions, again adding unnecessary weight. The original specification of 117.5 inches (2.98m) was soon joined by an optional long-wheelbase chassis of 130 inches (3.30m), which at once outsold the original. Later models were bigger still, culminating in no less than 156 inches (3.96m) for the longer version of the magnificent 8 Litre.

Let us imagine that by some magic power we can transport ourselves back into the 1920s, so that we can examine these gorgeous Bentleys in their original state. To help our chance of finding some examples, we shall aim to arrive in the London area, since more owners by far lived in that region than anywhere else. When we spot one, the chances of it being a tourer – say one of the Vanden Plas versions with which we are so familiar today – are quite small. Much more likely is that we shall come across a closed car – say, a Weymann-style saloon from Freestone & Webb, or a formal limousine from H J Mulliner. Possibly we might see, parked down a

Since this Gurney Nutting Three Litre saloon, on chassis 405, dates from the end of 1923, it must be one of the very first Weymann-style bodies made by that firm. It was only during that year that the first UK licences were issued under the Weymann patents.

By contrast, Freestone & Webb stuck to traditional coachbuilding methods with this Three-Litre tourer from early 1925. The registration, XX 3115, can be discerned, but the chassis number is unknown. Note the separate screen for the rear passengers.

side-street, a luxurious four-seater with its hood erected, which its owner might refer to as a cabriolet or an all-weather. Passing in the distance might be a drophead coupé, with a third passenger in its dickey-seat, or a landaulet with its rear hood lowered.

Why are we finding it so difficult to find tourers? Clearly because there were fewer of them made, relative to the other body styles. And if that it so, why is it that in our own day there are so many tourers and so few of any other style? Part of the answer is that the more luxurious body styles – saloons, limousines, cabriolets – were much more difficult to keep in good order than were tourers. The luxury cars had a more complex wooden framework which flexed and creaked, and had more weight in the bodywork to assist that flexing. Worse, particularly with the saloons and limousines, is that they need to have much of their panelling removed before any framework repairs can be carried out. With a tourer, on the other hand, the framing and panelling is of much smaller dimensions, and repairs are correspondingly more affordable. Over the years, therefore, it is not surprising that it has been the closed bodies which have been scrapped first.

However that is not the whole story. Today there are many tourers in existence which started life as something else, usually a saloon or limousine. When an unrepairable body has been removed from a chassis, the obvious style with which to replace it is of course a tourer, usually a Vanden Plas-style replica. There is nothing wrong with this practice, provided the original body is truly beyond repair. On the other hand there have been many instances where a perfectly salvageable closed body has been sacrificed to the owner's desire for an open one. The motivation of these owners is perhaps understandable, but the result is one less example of a closed car to pass on to the next generation.

Because of the lack of variety in coachwork to be found on vintage Bentleys today, there is a danger that – whisper it not – we might even begin to find them dull! There are only so many Vanden Plas four-door tourers to be seen, lined up in rows at club meetings, before we might just begin to tire of their uniform magnificence. We can only hear so many times the story of these cars, or others just like them, carrying all before them in sports-car races of the 1920s. How refreshing it is when we come across, say, a saloon or a limousine, and can fantasise

It is said that W O introduced the 6½ Litre chassis precisely to cope with massive bodies such as this limousine. This Vanden Plas body probably dates from 1926. Note the vee-windscreen, shortly to go out of fashion.

H J Mulliner bodied many vintage Bentley chassis. This is a drophead coupé on Three Litre chassis 1093 from mid-1925, typical of the period with its long tail containing a dickey-seat (and probably a vestigial luggage-boot).

From the same period – mid-1926 – is another very early 6½ Litre (note the lack of bonnet louvres), given the treatment by Freestone & Webb. This is a Weymann saloon on chassis WB 2557. Ship-type scuttle ventilators were a must-have item at the time.

about its first owner and the life which that car led: shopping in Town, maybe, or taking the family to Ascot or to Brooklands.

Even before the first owner took delivery there would have been the weeks of anticipation while its precise form of bodywork was decided, with the coachbuilder's wash drawings studied closely and then a detailed specification drawn up. What colour should the outside panels be? Which colour and weave of cloth to choose for the interior? Then the wait, and probably the inspection visits, while the body was being constructed, at Gurney Nutting's Chelsea premises, maybe, or Park Ward's at Willesden. If the family employed a chauffeur, he would have been made familiar with the intricacies of the car well before it was delivered.

And who were these coachbuilders? Many of them had of course been in existence as carriage-builders,

This Three Litre drophead coupé is thought to date from around 1926, and is by Page & Hunt of Farnham, Surrey (predecessors to Abbott). Note the rear window pillars, which appear to be hinged so that they drop down when the car is in the fully open position.

As a means of uprating the power of the Three Litre without going to the extent of six cylinders, Bentley introduced the 4½ Litre model in 1927. It was an obvious candidate for the standard Vanden Plas tourer treatment, as shown in this 1928 photo. Note that a driver's door was still not considered essential.

and were dripping with craftmanship and tradition. At the beginning of the 20th century there were countless firms – certainly thousands – dotted up and down the land who were capable of building a carriage from scratch, and who attempted to adapt their skills to building bodies for motor cars. Some of them succeeded, while others gave up and were content merely to carry out repair work. As the years went by new firms, just as competent technically, sprang up to satisfy the growing demands of the automobile industry. By the time the Bentley car appeared on the scene, some of the newer firms (Gurney Nutting, Park Ward) had established reputations just as prestigious as the more traditional ones (H J Mulliner, Vanden Plas).

Well over a hundred different coachbuilders are known to have bodied at least one vintage Bentley. In practice, however, the large firms located in west and north-west London had the lion's share of the work. Indeed the top six firms – the four mentioned above, plus Freestone & Webb and Harrison – accounted for nearly two-thirds of the 3024 chassis produced. If there was a common factor amongst these six firms, in addition to their general competence, it was their design skills. The 1920s was the era when the ability of sheer looks to influence sales first became evident to both coachbuilders and – later – to the chassis manufacturers. Up to that point a coachbuilder's prowess had been judged largely on quality of workmanship. Increasingly, though, as the 1920s unfolded this was coupled with the ability to produce designs which were inherently attractive to the eye. Skill such as this often rested in the hands of one man, whose name

The standard of workmanship involved, particularly in closed bodies, can be judged from the veneered panelwork on this door. This is the Vanden Plas 1926 Olympia Show car, a limousine on 6½ Litre chassis FW2605.

Also from 1928 is this 4½ Litre Weymann saloon from Freestone & Webb. The dummy stretchers ("pram irons") on the rear quarter were a popular affectation at the time, and led to the description "faux [false] cabriolet". Note the arrival of the peaked roof, soon to become even more exaggerated.

Vanden Plas built this two-seater racer in mid-1928, presumably to a customer's specific order, on 4½ Litre chassis XL3124. It demonstrates how ideas about "streamlining" – in other words, reducing air-resistance – were beginning to take hold in public consciousness.

in many cases has lived on in timeless examples of coachwork design.

Another intriguing question is why these different body styles existed at all. That they all started from horse-and-carriage equivalents is certainly true, but it does not get us very far. The early years of the motor car saw a rapid evolution in coachwork design, to take account of the car's very different requirements compared with the horse-drawn age. Weather protection, in particular, was a far more important subject when the vehicle was travelling at 30 or 40 miles per hour instead of 10. Only gradually, however, did the various specialised types of coachwork emerge.

The coupé de ville style was to many the ultimate symbol of luxury, and it was therefore usually to be found on the more expensive chassis. Gurney Nutting's version shown here, on 6½ Litre chassis KF2378 of early 1929, is in the latest fashion with its cycle wings, dummy hood irons and steps instead of running-boards. Although it is hard to tell from the photo, it was probably built on "semi-Weymann" principles.

Vanden Plas were not users of the semi-Weymann system, preferring instead to take a "British Flexible " licence from Harrison. This 6½ Litre saloon (chassis WT2260) was probably built in this manner. Note that there is now a trunk for luggage rather than a folding rack.

The Bristol Aeroplane company were far from well-known as coachbuilders, but their Weymann saloon shown here is quite stylish. It is on Speed Six chassis BA2582, and dates from early1929. Note an early use of glass window-louvres.

This Gurney Nutting Speed Six is virtually a two-seater, the small third seat being arranged crosswise in the back. An early example of a "fastback", it adds to its sportiness with louvred chassis valances. The chassis is HM2855 from mid-1929. It is remarkable for its very advanced styling, facilitated by Gurney-Nutting's use of aluminium castings for the windscreen and front window pillars.

Freestone & Webb also attempted a sporting body on a Speed Six chassis (LR2790, mid-1930), and it was not their most outstanding design. It said the right things, with its helmet wings and float-type running-boards, and it even had the hint of a falling waistline, a feature which became popular during the 1930s.

Limousines and saloons, the latter lacking a glass division between passengers and driver, were perhaps the styles which most resembled their horse-and-carriage antecedents. This is understandable, since in both eras there was a clear requirement from certain buyers for a totally closed vehicle. Others evolved from previous variants such as landaus (totally open if required) or landaulets (only partially open). These gave perfectly satisfactory service in the horse-drawn era, but were found wanting in one respect or another when coach-builders built them on motor-car chassis. Gradually they mutated, through versions known as all-weathers and cabriolets, to the more familiar sports, tourer and drophead coupé styles.

Another legacy from the carriage-building era was the manner in which automobile bodies were constructed. The coachbuilder began by building up a wooden framework, almost always of ash, on which the panels could be fixed. These panels were initially also of wood, usually mahogany or walnut, and were carefully shaped and fitted into the rebated framework. Blacksmiths, painters, trimmers, fine-liners, varnishers and so on then completed the work. Given the amount of hand labour involved, and particularly bearing in mind the long drying times needed for each of the many coats of paint and varnish, it is understandable that production times were quoted in months rather than weeks.

From quite early on the wooden panels became metal – usually steel, but often aluminium. The size of individual panels increased, too, particularly as welding techniques became more sophisticated. In most other respects, however, the general approach to building a body changed very little until the early 1920s. At that point the introduction of the Weymann system represented a significant change, even though it still used a wooden frame. However not all coachbuilders, by any means, adopted the Weymann method. Their reluctance to change was vindicated, to an extent, by the arrival of a second revolutionary development – cellulose painting. This process did away with a huge amount of time and effort in the paint shop, and opened the way to

The Eight Litre chassis was lower than that of previous models, and it inspired coachbuilders to produce some very elegant designs. This is H J Mulliner's 1930 Olympia Show car, a limousine on chassis YF5006, so well-proportioned that its sheer size is not immediately apparent.

These last two photos illustrate the convergence of drophead coupé and tourer styles at the end of the decade. The first, on Eight Litre chassis YX5111 from May 1932, Vanden Plas described as a "tourer". Yet it has only two doors and might even have wind-up windows, although the driver's door may be cutaway.

much shorter timescales in bodybuilding. Even then, coachbuilt, as opposed to mass-production, bodies continued to be built up from individual panels mounted on a wooden framework.

The fundamental problem with the "coachbuilt" method was, as we have seen, that the bodywork could not withstand the stresses imposed on it by the twisting and bending of the chassis. As the 1920s ended, coachbuilders were starting to make great strides in finding a solution, both by increasing the ability of the framework to resist these stresses and by insulating it better from the chassis. Unfortunately none of these developments arrived during the production life of the vintage Bentley. The result, as we have seen, is that most of the original bodies have been scrapped long ago.

So although examples of different body styles on vintage Bentleys still exist, they are few and far between. If we want to see how things were in the 1920s, we can of course photograph these examples, and indeed this is what has been done for this book.

I am very grateful to the owners of these five cars for their cooperation. They are Humphrey Avon, Brian Bashall and Brian Baskerville, plus one other who wishes to remain anonymous. In addition, however, we are fortunate in having to hand numerous photographs taken at the time. We have drawn on this store as widely as possible, to help us trace the evolution of the different body styles through the 1920s and to celebrate the true diversity of coachwork which appeared on the vintage Bentley. Many of these photographs are from the archive of that supreme Bentley expert, Tim Houlding. I should like to record my sincere thanks to Tim not only for making that archive available but also for much additional assistance while I was preparing this book.

Nick Walker *Ilmington, April 2005*

The second, by Park Ward in mid-1931 on an Eight Litre chassis, number YR5093, was described as a "drophead coupé" – and it bears all the necessary characteristics, such as two doors and wind-up windows.

Chapter One

Saloons and Limousines

We have all become so used to the sight of vintage Bentleys with open, usually tourer, bodies that we overlook how important saloons and limousines were when the cars were new. Yet for expensive cars of this sort the closed body was much more the norm, being the lineal descendant of the closed carriage of 30 years previously. And just as a person of substance would have ordered a bespoke design of closed carriage in the 19th century, so in the 20th century it seemed perfectly natural for him to visit his coachbuilder and commission a bespoke design of saloon or limousine body.

Even as late as 1919, the well-known motoring columnist Owen John commented on this heritage. "One of the foremost of motor manufacturing firms in this country is advertising to the effect that the prices of its chassis are so much, and the bodies can be made as their customers please by their 'family coachbuilders'... The family coachbuilder is a conservative person, and it is a long and hard task to get him to give up altogether many of his past glories in the matter of scrolls and ledges and curves and all the gilded panoply that went with cocked hats and padded calves."

It is no surprise, therefore, that the coachbuilding methods of the 1920s were closely related to carriage-building techniques developed in the previous century. Indeed one could speculate that the whole idea of producing only a chassis, and then farming it out to another firm altogether to build a body on it, would never have been contemplated if the legacy of horse-and-carriage practice had not been in existence. However that was the way one did things in the early 1920s, and W O Bentley was in no position to force through a different approach even if he had wanted to do so. On the contrary, launching a new and expensive marque of car was such a risky business anyway that he would have tried any means to capture the "carriage trade" (as it was still called in those days). How better than by offering them a large and powerful chassis on which they could build their ideal body?

Having said that, it is well known that W O perceived his creation as primarily a sporting vehicle, and would have preferred his customers to have added lightweight, open bodywork rather than heavy saloons or limousines. However, he was in no position to enforce such a preference; indeed the demand for "town" coachwork soon forced him to offer longer wheelbase chassis to accommodate those customers who felt that the standard chassis did not afford them sufficient room. Thus it was that this great sporting marque was as often seen, when it was new, in the form of a closed car as an open one.

At the time that Bentley chassis started to come off the production line in late 1921, the typical coachbuilt body, whether closed or open, would have been constructed in very much the same way. A framework of stout, seasoned ash timbers, carefully jointed one to the other, was built up from the chassis. The "bottom sides" – the heavy longitudinal members supporting the framework at each side of the car – were securely attached to the chassis at numerous points. This structure was then covered in hand-beaten panels of either steel or aluminium. The panels in turn might then have been welded into a "one-piece" body, but more likely the joints between them were covered by moulding pieces.

Then came the painting stage. The traditional coach-painting process at that time was a laborious matter of laying on successive layers of primers, fillers, guide coat, stopping coat, "common colour" and "best colour" – each one by hand, and each one having a long drying time – followed by the fearful business of hand-varnishing. This was fraught with the risk of dust entering the atmosphere before the varnish had dried, and both coachbuilders and volume manufacturers used filtering and other tricks to minimise it. A coachbuilder described in 1921 just what the pressures were on his coach-painting department: the "ideal" process, using all the successive coats desirable, would take no less than 48 working days, and even what he termed a "practical" sequence took 20 days. "When a customer asks how long it will take to paint his body, the answer from the foreman coach-painter is always 'Oh, 20 to 30 days', whereas in practice the shop could not afford to take so long".

After painting, the body went into the trim shop, where highly-skilled craftsmen did their best to turn the interior of the body – particularly if it was a closed one – into a passable imitation of the customer's living-room. Whereas the chauffeur had to make do with stiff, waterproof leather, his passengers would be seated on the finest West of England cloth, surrounded by inlaid wooden panels, Axminster carpeting, blinds with silk pulls and cut-glass perfume bottles in the "lady's companion set". The large expanse of space in front of the rear seats could be filled, if necessary, by occasional seats which folded out from the floor or from the division between passengers and driver.

We should take the opportunity at this point to make the distinction between saloons and limousines. Both have fixed roofs, and both normally have four doors; the difference is that a limousine has a division between the passengers' and driver's compartments. This division extends all the way between floor and roof, the upper part being glass which can be slid sideways, swung up or wound down when one wants to communicate with the driver. Occasional seats, too, are typical of limousines; often they faced rearwards, in another reminder of carriage-building practice.

Although large amounts of foot-room were the norm in both saloons and limousines in the 1920s, the space would have been even more massive in a limousine. This tradition again went back to horse-and-carriage days, where it was common for the luggage to be placed inside at the passengers' feet in order to protect it from the weather. Not that carrying luggage was regarded as a proper function for a limousine, since it was normally used as a town carriage; accompanying luggage would have been picked up separately, probably by a carrier's cart.

Some limousines condescended to offer a fold-out luggage-grid for emergency use, but even then it was often concealed behind an anonymous panel in the tail. The coachbuilding expert Herbert Butler, writing in 1924, put the matter bluntly: "A true town carriage requires neither roof rail nor luggage rack. If these are required for station work, they should be made easily removable so as to enhance the appearance of the equipage when it is being used for paying calls, or driving in the park." His reference to roof rails harks back to a common feature of pre-WW1 cars, which often had a strengthened roof which could hold luggage. This practice soon disappeared after the war, to the great relief of both body and chassis designers – the former because their bodies had to be far more rigid than was otherwise necessary, the latter because the extra weight of such bodies had a dire effect on their cars' performance. It is probably also true that the inertia of the luggage at such a height above the car's centre of gravity would have accentuated any tendency to sway during cornering, shortening the life of the framework joints and hence of the body as a whole.

This question of the life of a closed body brings us to one of the fundamental problems facing coachbuilders from the early days of the motor car. While their closed carriages had lasted for generations in many cases, the motorised equivalent began to squeak and rattle within a very short time. The cause is not hard to find: the sorts of speeds that a car could attain, and the consequent stresses on its chassis, were far greater than a horse-drawn carriage normally experienced. Open bodies were far less prone to this type of damage, since their lack of a roof structure meant that they could comply more easily with any chassis distortion.

Thus the builders of closed bodies, in particular, faced the twin – and to some extent linked – problems of weight and flexing. The former sapped the inherent performance of the chassis; the latter led initially to squeaks and rattles, and eventually to more serious problems – splitting in the panels, cracked or broken glass, and eventually the scrapping of the whole body. They therefore set about trying to solve both problems as a matter of urgency. However, there was at this stage no agreement as to what an ideal body mounting method might be. An article at the time (1922) seriously suggested that the most effective solution would be to suspend the body from each corner by leather straps and C-springs, presumably as coaches used to be in the last century, and that only cost considerations prevented this method being adopted.

The initial solution was to try and insulate the body from the flexing of the chassis by use of a subframe insulated by some elastic medium, either rubber or spring steel. A great deal of ingenuity was devoted to such systems throughout the decade, and indeed into the 1930s. Daimler, still building some although far from all of their own bodies, were devotees from pre-war days of a subframe system; theirs used a patented steel frame, hinged at the rear and with rubber buffers at the front.

The Lanchester version used a form of double insulation, in that the body was separated by rubber washers from mounting brackets, which in turn were also rubber-insulated from the chassis. Later (1925) both Connaught and James Young brought out their own variants; Connaught's, shown at Olympia that year, used a four-point mounting, while the James Young five-point version, using Hardy Spicer flexible discs, was even more complex. A contemporary report explained how it coped with an increasingly common problem, a body which is much wider than the chassis: "A rigid bar of channel steel is bolted across the chassis, and the disc is connected to this bar instead of direct to the chassis, which naturally gives the same effect. With this system of mounting, it is essential that scuttle separation is employed, a rubber tube being used with two flanges, one on either side, one flange being fixed to the body scuttle and the other to the dashboard. When the chassis distorts on the road, stresses are not transmitted direct to the body, but are absorbed in the disc, thus reducing the wear and rattle that are wont to develop in door locks, dovetails and handles. Owing to the fact that the weight of the passengers and seats is resting direct on the chassis, the discs are called upon to carry comparatively little weight."

Other coachbuilders approached the problem by trying to make their body frames even more rigid, so that they could better resist the flexing of the chassis – in effect, add to the combined rigidity of the chassis-body unit. To achieve this, many tried reinforcing their frames with steel at critical points, and there were even some early attempts at all-steel framework. However, before either sub-frames or steel reinforcement could gain wide acceptance there arrived a radical alternative, namely the Weymann method of construction. We shall be discussing Weymann later, but it is worth noting at this point that it was introduced with the twin objectives of reducing weight and eliminating squeaks and rattles; prolonging the life of the bodywork, whilst certainly a third advantage, was regarded as a by-product.

So we can begin to see why so many W O Bentley chassis received closed bodywork, and yet why so few of these bodies have survived. The type of customer who could afford a Bentley was attracted to the idea of a sporting car, but nevertheless felt that he needed the respectability offered by a limousine or saloon. Yet that type of body, far from being a wise purchase, was the least able to stand up to normal wear and tear. Our customer was probably not too concerned, since he probably changed his car every two years on principle, but on the second-hand market a thirsty, rattling saloon would soon run out of buyers.

What did an early-1920s closed car look like? Some of its features were dictated by the chassis manufacturer and were common to all types of body. For example, at the beginning of the decade manufacturers were still wedded to low bonnets and high scuttles, exactly as before the war. (The name "scuttle", incidentally, was a shortened form of "scuttle-dash", so called when a designer covered the flat dashboard with a curved panel, and a journalist likened the resultant shape to a scuttle.) Windscreens were usually large, flat panels, although the vee-type was making headway, and large-diameter wire wheels bore spindly beaded-edge tyres. Door-handles were the "ring" type, as on railway carriages of the period, and their windows were raised by the strap-and-peg system.

Limousines, in particular, were often characterised by having the driver's compartment open to the elements. Usually this meant no side-windows, but in some cases there was no roof either. The rapid disappearance of this brutal treatment of the driver over the first years of the decade might charitably be ascribed to a concern for the chauffeur's welfare. However, it was also related to the increased number of "owner-drivers", which occurred after the war even at this elevated end of the market. Coachbuilders took to describing such bodies as "enclosed drive", to distinguish them from what had previously been the norm. Surprisingly, there had been some initial resistance to this feature from both coachbuilders and manufacturers, including Herbert Austin who before World War 1 said that the body in which the driver's seat is "closed in" was "probably the most difficult type to build satisfactorily". His implication was that such a design was even more prone to twisting, and therefore joint flexing, than one which stopped behind the front seat.

By the time the first Bentleys were put on sale, fashion in closed cars was already showing some change. It has to be admitted that these models were the least affected by aesthetic considerations – unlike, that is, the more flamboyant drophead coupés and tourers, where the appearance of the finished product was starting to have an effect on a buying decision. As far as saloons and limousines went, comfort would always take pride of place over appearance, as witness this description of a Gurney Nutting offering at the 1922 London Show: "An interior drive saloon is fitted to a Bentley, and is noticeable for the extreme cosiness of the interior, the crimson upholstery being most inviting and warm-looking, while the cushioning is also very comfortably and luxuriously arranged". Nevertheless we can begin to trace attempts to improve the appearance of saloons and limousines during the early part of the decade.

As a generalisation, the 1920s were the decade when manufacturers realised that looks could sell - in other words that car buyers were far more influenced by a car's appearance than they would admit to, or indeed were even aware of themselves. Nowhere was this more clearly understood than in America, where the principle of annual cosmetic model changes was established at General Motors as early as 1925. Already at that date there were some 17 million cars in use in the United States, and to sell more was increasingly a matter of persuading existing owners to change to a new model.

Even in Europe, though, the concept of making a car's appearance "attractive" – whatever that word meant at the time – through careful body design was increasingly understood as the decade progressed. The difference from America was that in Europe it carried more weight at the expensive end of the market, where the decision was which car to have rather than whether one could afford a car at all. Thus the bespoke coachbuilding industry carried the burden, far more than volume manufacturers, of pioneering new body styles.

It took time for this realisation – that customers would respond favourably to designs that were aesthetically pleasing – to make its mark on the coachbuilding industry, and even then it had to be applied with caution. There can be little doubt that the typical British buyer was conservative in his views, certainly more so than his Continental counterpart, and so innovations in design had to be introduced little by little. Gradually, though, spurred on in part by changes in the artistic and design environment at the time, the form of the coachbuilt product began to change, and with it in due course the corresponding designs from volume manufacturers. Nevertheless, the rate of change only accelerated towards the end of the decade, and reached its full flowering in the 1930s.

Closed cars, in particular, had a notably angular appearance at the start of the decade. Gradually, though, designers began to make changes. Corners, for example, starting with the corner where the rear panel joined the roof, began to be rounded off. At the same time the roof itself changed from being almost flat to being perceptibly domed. This was not only for appearance's sake, but also to help reduce the drumming noise to which flat roofs were particularly prone. Even this was not sufficient, however, and later it became common both to line the roof with a sound-absorbent material and to cover it externally with fabric. Small, steel-panel ventilators had been fitted to roofs since before the war, mainly, it is said, to allow the escape of gentlemen's cigarette smoke. During the 1920s they became a virtually standard fitting to saloons and limousines, often being made of glass in order to lighten the somewhat gloomy interior.

Gradually, too, the vee-windscreen ousted the large area of flat glass. Some traced this back to the adoption of "enclosed drive"; the chauffeur's compartment now required some ventilation to avoid the screen misting up, but it was only necessary for half of the screen to have the facility. Soon afterwards someone realised that one could have this feature without a vee configuration, and flat two- or three-panel screens became the norm. It was also found helpful to provide a "peak" (an extension of the roof) which projected in front of the windscreen and shaded the driver's eyes from the sun. The side windows soon lost their strap-and-peg lifting system in favour of one of the new types of patent window-lift – Rawlings, Perfecta or

Hobson – which used a winding-handle instead. The driver's window was made of two sliding panels, or alternatively embodied a quick-lift device, either of which allowed him to open and close the window rapidly for signalling. Most importantly of all, the bonnet line was raised to the same level as the waist (known to coachbuilders as the belt-rail), with a profoundly beneficial effect on the appearance of the car.

Somewhere around 1923 the "balloon" tyre, with its fatter section, became a standard fitment, greatly improving the appearance of all cars, closed or open. At the same time there began a fashion for disc wheels, which would later die out before returning in a different form in the 1930s. At the same time the vee-windscreen fashion began to die out. The newer designs were not only flat, but sloping as well, often to match up with a sloping door-pillar line. They also changed gradually from being split horizontally, with the top half opening, to the one-piece version which opened in its entirety from a hinge at the top.

We said earlier that we would return to the subject of the Weymann system. While developments such as sub-frames had been proceeding, a wholly different approach to the twin problems of weight and flexing had arrived on the scene from France. Why, mused M Weymann, try to make your bodywork more and more rigid? Instead, make it flexible, let it ride with the twists and turns of the chassis, and let anything of importance, especially seats, be mounted directly on the chassis, independent of the body. The bodywork's sole function, in effect, would be to protect the passengers from the elements, and hence it could be made both flexible and much lighter. Thus was the Weymann system born: a light, cellular wooden frame covered with padding and fabric ("imitation leather"). In later versions there were also aluminium panels, or sometimes expanded metal, to give curved rather than square corners.

As well as dramatically lightening a conventional body - maybe by as much as 50%, which would typically mean 3-4 cwt (150 -200kg) - the system "eliminated" squeaks and rattles from the framework. It did this by introducing a gap of 4-6mm between the members of every joint, these being held together, or rather apart, by metal plates. To give an idea of the detailed development which eventually went into the system, each plate was itself separated from its wooden member by a strip of grease-proof paper, and fixing was not by wood-screws but by counter-sunk bolts and nuts. In the few cases where it was not possible to avoid wood contacting wood, such as in fabricating certain complicated shapes, then leather or canvas was inserted between the two parts. Similarly, felt was used between the bottom bars and the chassis when the body was mounted. The whole assembly was covered in leather-cloth; the space between the outer covering and the interior lining was sometimes filled with cotton wool or horse-hair. Doors were not a tight fit, but instead shut on to soft seals; the doors themselves were extremely flexible, and were fitted internally with straining wires to allow their shape to be adjusted if necessary. The lightness of the structure also allowed it to be built out beyond the width of the chassis, in order to give more room in the passenger compartment.

The claim was that the body would remain absolutely silent even after long service - something that was especially desirable in France with its pavé surfaces. As a bonus, its light fabric roof also solved the problem of drumming, which plagued the owners of steel-roofed saloons for most of the decade (and which was probably cured through the widespread adoption of the sunshine roof). A further claimed advantage was that these bodies were much easier to keep clean, and compared with the varnished paintwork then in use it was certainly true. Although early versions tended to be rather square in shape, users of the system soon found ways of adding curvature at the right places, to the point where a Weymann body and a coachbuilt one looked very similar in outline. The one difference – and a major one in the end – was the matt surface finish of the Weymann.

As far as Britain was concerned, the first news of this impending revolution arrived in the early part of 1923. This was a description of the system, followed by the announcement of the start of full production in Paris (although it would appear that development work had begun as early as 1920). Incidentally, it is a telling comment on the insularity of the coachbuilding trade at that time that the motorist could find out much more about Weymann from his weekly magazine than the professional could from his monthly journal. Learning from their experience in France, where they made all their own bodies and were hard put to keep up with their growth rate, Weymann decided in Britain that licensing was to be their initial way forward (this was also a means of keeping their initial capital investment to a minimum). While the first two licences in 1923 appear to have been granted to car manufacturers –

Talbot-Darracq and Rover – the first to a coachbuilder was probably for a Bentley, when Chalmer & Hoyer (forerunners of Hoyal) produced a four-door saloon body on a Three Litre Bentley chassis. This claim might have been disputed by Elkington, who obtained a licence at about the same time to produce a saloon body on a Peugeot 12.

Chalmer & Hoyer exhibited their pioneering Weymann body at the 1923 Olympia Show, and it attracted considerable attention. This is from *The Motor*: "A body of considerable interest is a four-door 5-seater saloon on a Three Litre Bentley constructed under the Weymann principles and patents. It has adjustable front seats, frameless windows and mechanical window lifters, while the body is panelled in leather cloth. A feature of the Weymann system ... is that the body flexes with the chassis and that it is absolutely rattle-proof." By the next year's Show Cadogan, Gurney Nutting, and Windover had been added to the list, and Freestone & Webb are also known to have had a licence by then. In 1925 Harrington and H J Mulliner, among many others, joined the list of licensees.

The Bentley company were whole-hearted supporters of the Weymann system. Their 1925 catalogue offered as standard a "Flexible Saloon", with the following accompanying text: "A highly developed form of flexible body has been produced, based on the Weymann patents. This construction is effected on the principle that the body shall be flexible and a special fabric employed instead of the normal metal scuttle and body panels. The advantages obtained are a great saving in weight, remarkable silence after prolonged wear, and a minimum of labour to keep clean. A good variety both of colours and surface finish is available, from which a choice of panel fabric can be made."

There was a certain amount of scepticism in Britain as to whether Weymann bodies would be accepted. W F Bradley, continental correspondent of *The Autocar*, expressed it clearly. "If Weymann had endeavoured to develop this idea in England he would have got no further than his first experimental model. The English motorist would have cast a glance at the dull, box-like structure, and would have remarked: 'It may be light, but it is ugly; it may be silent, but my beautiful coach body is not noisy; it may be enduring, but experience has taught us that endurance can only be obtained by strength, and I could break some of those flimsy frame members over my knee', and that would have been the end of Weymann's idea in England."

In the event, the Weymann system took both France and Britain by storm. In Britain, the company achieved increasing success until the late years of the 1920s, although the peak was somewhat earlier in France. While the British company's policy of licensing continued, they decided to build bodies themselves as well, and in 1925 moved into a factory in Putney; they soon outgrew it, and in 1928 moved again to Addlestone. While numbers are hard to come by, it is known that in France in their best years of 1926-7 some 12,000 Weymann bodies were produced, and that the British figures, while somewhat lower, were of the same order. It is therefore possible that, at a very rough estimate, Weymann bodies formed a third of all British coachbuilt production in these peak years. At the 1928 Olympia Show 37% of the exhibits had fabric bodies, mostly Weymanns. Certainly it was claimed in 1928 that there were 50,000 Weymann bodies in use in the two countries combined. By that time, though, the system's attractions had been whittled away by numerous competitors, as we shall see later.

Many were the coachbuilding firms who built Weymann saloons on Bentley chassis, but probably the three most prolific were Freestone & Webb, Gurney Nutting and Vanden Plas. The first two were young organisations, having been founded after the War. In the former case both V E Freestone and A J Webb were experienced men; Freestone came from the Crossley company, and had previously been with a provincial coachbuilder in Sevenoaks in Kent, while Webb is said to have come from a "French coachbuilder", quite possibly the Sizaire-Berwick or De Dion Bouton coachbuilding departments in London. They started operating in 1923 from premises in Willesden, which were to remain home to the Freestone & Webb business for the whole of its existence. Within their first year they were bodying Bentleys, and only a year later had taken out a Weymann licence.

From that moment on the Freestone & Webb Weymann saloon on the Three Litre Bentley typified the marque's image in its early years, with its sharp corners gradually becoming rounded off as Weymann techniques became more sophisticated. There is some justification for the view that their designs became a little more ordinary as the decade progressed, and this may be connected with the company's financial problems which ended in Freestone's departure. Nevertheless their contribution to Bentley's vintage era was immense. They are known to have bodied 239 chassis (the great majority Weymann saloons), making them the fourth most prolific coachbuilder for the marque.

J Gurney Nutting, by contrast, was a coach-building novice when he decided to compete in 1919. His firm, incredibly, were builders and joiners, who had built army huts during the War, a source of business which obviously disappeared overnight. Nothing daunted, he purchased the Marlborough Carriage Works in Croydon, South London, and began to build car bodies. His success was breathtaking. Although he had a setback when his Croydon works burnt down in 1924, he turned even that to advantage by moving into the fashionable Chelsea district of London.

From the outset Gurney Nutting concentrated on coachwork with a sporting flavour, and they were particularly associated with the Bentley marque. They had built their first Bentley body even before the move to London. Thereafter they became, after Vanden Plas, the Cricklewood firm's next biggest supplier of bodies, reaching a total of 362 by 1931. Many of these were built under Weymann patents, the firm having embraced the system from as early as 1924.

When Gurney Nutting saloons found royal customers – Prince Albert (later King George VI) in 1926 and Prince George (later the Duke of Kent) in 1926 and 1929 – it did their reputation no harm at all. The firm's greatest asset was its designer, A F McNeil, and as the decade progressed his designs increasingly showed the flair which would blossom fully during the 1930s.

Vanden Plas, by contrast, went back to before World War 1; indeed their Belgian predecessors were carriage-builders in the 19th century. Their association with the Bentley company began in 1922 and, in spite of a financial reconstruction in 1923, remained close for the rest of the decade, with Bentley leasing part of the Vanden Plas premises for their service department. They bodied far more Bentley chassis – 662 – than any other coachbuilder.

Although these days we tend to associate the Vanden Plas name more with open Bentley bodies, particularly tourers, they were also prolific builders of luxury saloons and limousines. This is their 1924 Olympia Show exhibit: "Here we find an example of comfort and luxury without extravagance in appearance. A light grey and black saloon on a long-chassis Bentley is shown with silver-plated fittings and the interior upholstered in antique dark brown furniture hide, suggesting solid comfort and long wearing qualities. It has six windows and Triplex glass is used throughout."

Even more luxurious was their 1926 Show offering: "A single example of coachwork is staged. It is a magnificent limousine mounted on a long wheelbase six-cylinder Bentley. There is accommodation for seven passengers, two of whom occupy revolving seats, and every care has been taken to ensure the maximum of comfort – witness the interior heating of the back compartment, the well-proportioned seats and the wide doors. The heating, by the way, is easily controlled by a small lever that can be reached without leaving the back seat. It is a four-door, six-light body, and all the windows may be lowered. Triplex glass is used throughout. Both interior and exterior convey an impression of good taste; the fittings are beautifully made, and the 'café au lait' in which all the exterior is painted is most taking. The price complete of this fine car is £2,500."

At the same time as the Weymann system began to be adopted, there were also signs of a development that would change the shape of cars probably more than any other single feature - the luggage boot. Initially it tended to be no more than a separate trunk, attached to the rear of the car, although Arthur Mulliner did manage (1924) to build space for four cases into the back of a D-back limousine. The following year Hill and Boll produced one of the very first sloping back treatments containing a luggage boot. These were the exceptions, however, and the norm – where luggage accommodation was provided at all – was the separate trunk, fixed to the body but looking as if it was detachable. This style became much more developed in France, so much so that it eventually gave its name to the "Continental coupé"; by 1927, indeed, there was acceptance even amongst British designers that the French were ahead in the matter of providing accommodation for luggage.

The British industry, however, soon recognised the pressures to provide covered space for luggage, even in relatively small cars, and the result was the "sportsman's coupé". This was a two-door, four-light style which arrived so quickly and from so many different coachbuilders that the 1928 Olympia was dubbed "the Show of the Sportsman's Coupé". By moving the rear passengers forward within the wheelbase, often by making room for their feet under the front seats, designers were able to add luggage space behind the rear seat, within the overall outline of the body. In many instances there was no external door to this space, access being gained by folding down the back seat.

The sportsman's coupé style found its way on to Bentleys, including a Gurney Nutting exhibit at the 1930 Olympia Show: "That the sportsman's coupé is definitely established as a body type, although it may not be so popular as formerly, is proved by the several examples at Olympia, one of the most attractive of which is to be seen on this stand on the new eight-litre Bentley chassis. The low build of the chassis has enabled a smart low-built appearance to be obtained without any sacrifice of comfort, and the proportions of the two-door, four-light body are to be admired. Incidentally, this is of panelled Weymann construction with a fixed head, and the colour scheme of fawn and black shows an unusual treatment. Bucket-type front seats are fitted, and the brown leather upholstery is comfortably carried out."

The interesting point about the more expensive saloons and (especially) limousines is that they resisted the trend to luggage trunks or boots longer than any other body-style (apart maybe from sports cars); instead they made do with a folding or concealed luggage-grid. There was a good reason: these were normally town cars, and on the rare occasions when they were employed on longer journeys the luggage would be sent on ahead, by rail, by steamer or in the second car with the staff. These cars were the last to retain the "D-back" shape of the early 1920s; other styles moved gradually to a straight, and then a sloping, shape of back in order to harmonise with the luggage trunk. At the same time the pronounced domed roof of the earlier years disappeared, in spite of its being less prone to drumming; no doubt this was not only for aesthetic reasons but also to accommodate the popular sliding roof.

This development – the sliding roof – was a highly sought-after feature on closed cars from the mid-1920s onwards. Without getting into a discussion as to when it was invented, it is certain that the design launched by coachbuilders Pytchley Autocar in 1925, and subsequently licensed to countless others, was the catalyst for its widespread adoption. Subsequently designs from SOS and Weathershields also became popular, not to mention various other proprietary devices such as the Kopalapso folding head, the Widney head, and the Tickford and Moorland fully-opening heads. These last two opened up the car so much that the style is better regarded as a form of cabriolet rather than a saloon.

This obsession with having the best of both worlds – fresh air or weather protection – was a particularly British phenomenon. An article in *The Motor* towards the end of the decade summarised the typical motorist's ambiguous feelings towards the subject: "One can perhaps understand a person with a delicate skin taking advantage of the ordinary saloon, but so far as others are concerned, surely in this country, where bright days are in the minority, one should make the most of them. The best way is, naturally, to have a touring car, but in view of our fickle climate and the fact that only one car per family generally is possible, the majority of owners run saloon cars. Why not, then, if you wish to make the most of our limited bright weather, go in for a compromise and purchase, or have your saloon converted into, a body of the open-air type?"

The writer then goes on to point out the virtues of such bodywork, including "making the most of the bright weather", "increasing one's range of vision" and "the ready facility with which the roof can be closed again." He then provides a word-portrait which brings the epoch to life before our eyes: "There is yet another point worth mentioning, this again being concerned with the motorist who would like two cars but cannot afford them. For instance, during the daytime, in the course of normal running, he prefers an open car, but in the evening time, when he and his wife are attending a dance, theatre or going out to dinner, an enclosed car naturally is preferable, especially as the lady invariably travels without her hat."

As well as the sliding roof, 1925 saw the arrival of a major technical innovation which was to have enormous influence on the appearance of coachwork thereafter. This was the cellulose painting process, which not only transformed volume manufacture by its speed of application, but also opened new opportunities for the specialist coachbuilders. Like so many other technical advances, it had been developed in America, and first used (by Cadillac and Oakland) as early as mid-1923. Its use was, of course, preceded by the perfection of paint-spraying techniques, which were being used with the older style lacquers before the arrival of cellulose. Indeed, Ford were using spraying at their Trafford Park factory as early as 1912, and it was in wide use by 1921, although it was more appropriate for simple components such as wings rather than the body itself. Dipping and flow-coating were also highly developed by 1922, and the larger factories were using "artificial drying" by 1924.

All these techniques, but especially the introduction of cellulose paint with its quick-drying properties, were aimed at cutting down the inordinate amount of time a body took to be painted. It is therefore surprising that the industry was rather slow to take up the cellulose process. Vanden Plas, with their aircraft-painting connections, and Lanchester claimed to be among the first users, which is likely to have been in 1925. Nevertheless, even though suppliers were advertising the product to the trade and offering use of their demonstration plants, only two other coachbuilders (Beadle and Short) were featuring cellulose finishes at Olympia that year. A year later it was still being treated as a novelty, and only by 1929 was it considered as near-universal. Needless to say, it was the more traditional end of the trade which was the slowest to make the change; even in 1928 Hooper were only conceding that "in some cases cellulose paint is used", before going on to describe lovingly the various stages of hand-painting.

Neither could any slowness in changing over to cellulose be blamed on the reluctance of the customer. It is hard for us to imagine from this distance the impact on a potential buyer when he saw a cellulose-painted car for the first time; its surface was as deeply lustrous as the finest hand-varnished product from an expensive coachbuilder, and its colour was many times brighter. More than that, though, it became apparent that its toughness allowed it to be cleaned easily without fear of scratching, something which could never have been said of varnish finishes. This was a significant point even at the bespoke end of the trade, at a time when chauffeurs were becoming less common and the owner-driver was unimpressed by the time and care necessary to look after the traditional type of paint-work. Furthermore, if an owner was unlucky enough to find a scratch, he could now in many instances polish it out, something which had not previously been possible.

The new range of bright colours available was soon exploited by coachbuilders. In place of the dark reds, dark blues and maroons which had previously been the norm, suddenly such colours as primrose, ivory and light blue began to appear; even the previously obligatory black wings became the same colour as the body. The gaiety of these colours seemed to capture the spirit of the age, a spirit which was unfortunately to change all too soon with the onset of the Depression. Later in the decade such colour combinations as yellow and brown, two shades of green or two shades of blue became popular, whereas by 1930 more sombre treatments such as greys and blacks were common.

Cellulose paints were probably responsible for the death of the Weymann body, and of all its fabric-covered imitators. Some loyal users of the system fought on, firstly by using cellulose paints themselves (so that they could at least compete on colour, if not on finish) and then by using the newly available glossy fabric known as "Tole Souple", which from a distance made the body look like one with coachbuilt metal panels. From contemporary accounts, incidentally, it would seem that Tole Souple was a very difficult material to work.

Another innovation was to apply dummy hood-irons to the rear quarters, thus giving the upper fabric the appearance of a drophead; this was the start of the many "faux cabriolet" (false cabriolet) treatments beloved of Continental coachbuilders in the 1930s. Nevertheless, buyers were not deceived. Fabric bodies were just not as attractive to look at as metal ones: they were dull instead of shiny, and they had sharp corners and flat panels instead of seductive curves.

One damning summary was that "some people live in tents and are satisfied; others prefer houses". Even their initial advantage of easy cleaning had been nullified by the advent of cellulose paints. On top of this, their general reputation had suffered at the hands of cheap imitators, since at the lower end of the market there were fabric bodies which were not noted for their longevity.

One design feature of the later 1920s for which the Weymann system can claim some credit is the "full-length door", where the door is carried right down to the running-board, obviating the need for a valance between the two. Certain coachbuilders (Hamshaw, Offord) had tried such a style in the early 1920s, but it was much easier to achieve with a Weymann body. This was not only because of the lightweight construction of the doors but also because, as we have seen, these bodies could easily be built out beyond the width of the chassis. Eventually, of course, the feature was copied by non-Weymann builders.

Running parallel with this development was another theme which was to dominate design thinking thereafter – the desire to reduce a car's overall height. Very probably this started as a result of early work on streamlining, but designers soon realised its aesthetic benefits. The key to achieving a lower profile was of course to seat the passengers lower, particularly those at the rear, and the quickest way to do this was to provide foot-wells for them. This feature, as we have noted previously, also allowed the rear seat to be moved forward within the wheelbase, and led directly to the emergence of the "sportsman's coupé". However, there was an alternative means of lowering seats in the car, namely by lowering the chassis. This was a more far-reaching development, which was not in the control of coachbuilders but required the cooperation of the manufacturers.

The manufacturers eventually responded to the entreaties of their coachwork suppliers, and underslung, downswept or "dropped" chassis became the norm by the end of the 1920s. What did not happen immediately, however, was a corresponding lowering of the bonnet line. Why this should have been the case is not totally clear; possibly there was a perceived need for the radiator header tank to be placed high up, even when many engines had moved from thermo-syphon cooling systems to pumped ones (by 1928, 67% of British production models had a water pump). Whatever the reason, retaining a high bonnet line meant retaining a high waist line as well, even though the roof had been lowered. Thus there came about the (shortlived) fashion for dramatically deep doors, surmounted by equally dramatic shallow windows - the "letter-box windscreen" era, as it has been called.

To modern eyes this trend is retrograde; it seems to be moving further from the low, balanced lines which became the norm in the 1930s. And there was more to come: the next fashion was for cycle wings. Their adoption was coupled with the removal of running-boards, since these no longer flowed naturally from the line of the wing. In most cases the running-board was replaced by a simple metal step, usually fixed but sometimes folding out when the door opened. The result was that the portions of the chassis members which had been concealed behind it were now revealed. Realising that even if the body width would permit it the current deep doors simply could not be deepened further to hide the chassis, designers instead found a new device, the chassis valance.

During the period that they were becoming lower, cars were also, towards the end of the 1920s, changing their interior layout. This was one of the most significant developments of the decade, and was triggered by a perceived need to accommodate the rear seats within the wheelbase. This was for a variety of reasons: primarily, as we have already seen, designers at this period were trying to incorporate the luggage-boot within the overall outline of the body. The result was a rash of "close-coupled" designs, initially the "sportsman's coupé", and then only a year or so later the "sportsman's saloon", a four-door/four-light style which was to some extent a reaction against the cramped access to the rear seat of the sportsman's coupé.

Other minor changes in design distinguished the later cars of the decade from their predecessors. The old style of moulding, often applied below side-windows, disappeared (to reappear in the next decade as a decorative, curved flash or swage-line). Inside, instrument panels suddenly took on an integrated appearance, instead of the dials being scattered all over the dashboard – leading, of course, to the indirectly illuminated dash. It also became common for saloons and limousines to be fitted with glass louvres over the side-windows, allowing them to be opened slightly without letting in rain or causing a draught.

Glass louvres were part of an increasing concern with the subject of ventilation. In the early part of the decade this was hardly a problem. Closed cars were not built for speed, and could manage with a simple roof ventilator for the passenger compartment. The driver's needs were taken care of by either an opening windscreen or indeed by sides open to the weather. As speeds increased, however, and as owner-drivers became the norm, something more sophisticated was required. Thus came scuttle ventilators, side-pillar ventilators, and eventually opening quarter-lights, initially only at the rear. Some coachbuilders began experimenting with heaters for the rear compartment, using the exhaust system as the source of heat.

After Weymann, there were other attempts to solve the problem of making the body flexible and yet retaining metal panels. One such was the "British Patent Flexible Fabric Body", developed by the coachbuilding firm of Harrison and Sons and launched at about the same time as the "semi-Weymann".

Harrison were a respected firm, established in 1883 and located in Stanhope Street, London NW1. They bodied almost 200 vintage Bentleys, and yet strangely never exhibited under their own name at the annual Olympia Motor Show. However, their close relations with the Bentley company are shown by the fact that their bodies adorned the exhibits on Bentley's Show stand on more than one occasion. It may well be that relations became too close, since Harrison ceased trading in the same year (1931) that Bentley went into receivership.

However, in 1927 everything was going swimmingly. That was the year they formed a separate subsidiary, British Flexible Coachworks Ltd, to promote their new system; interestingly, H M

Bentley (W O's brother) was a director of this company for a number of years. Here the flexibility was provided by sandwiching a layer of felt between the two halves of each joint of the framework, and then encasing the wood-screws which held the joint in rubber sleeves. Expanded metal was used on corners to help give a rounded shape. As with Weymann, the framework itself was very light and the floor and seats were fixed directly to the chassis. No doubt this would have been an attractive proposition to coachbuilders in the middle of the decade, but by the time it was introduced (1927) the swing against fabric bodies had begun, and as far as is known there is only one example – Vanden Plas – of a coachbuilder using the system under licence. It offered no particular advantages against the flexible, "semi-Weymann" method, and in any case was soon superseded by Silent Travel with its Silentbloc bushes.

The so-called "semi-Weymann" system attempted to exploit the attractiveness of cellulose-painted metal panels, by combining the usual Weymann lightweight frame and fabric covering for the upper half with metal cladding below the waist-line. Certain commentators at the time called into question the validity of trying to mix a flexible frame with rigid metal panels, but it would seem that they missed the fundamental basis of the revised Weymann method. This was to make the body frame act as a series of rigid cells, flexibly connected to each other. Thus the scuttle, rear quarter and doors were each in themselves rigid enough to take metal panelling, but their flexible connection to each other allowed the body as a whole to flex with the chassis as before. Relative movement between these "cells" was taken up by allowing the doors to move in two directions within the door-openings. The bottom-frames were jointed as before with metal plates, and care was taken to avoid trouble in critical places by not turning over the edges of the metal panels.

The semi-Weymann development undoubtedly gave a renewed impetus to the Weymann system, and to fabric bodies in particular. H J Mulliner made a speciality of this method of construction for a couple years, with numerous examples on Bentley chassis, whereas previously they had not been noted Weymann specialists.

Founded in 1900 by a member of the Northampton Mulliner family, the firm had quickly built a high reputation with their work on Rolls-Royce chassis. Soon after their move in 1906 from the centre of London to the suburb of Chiswick, the founder had sold out to the Edinburgh coachbuilders John Croall & Sons. However, this did nothing to dent their good name, and it was inevitable that they would body an expensive chassis such as the Bentley when it appeared. In all they bodied 248 vintage Bentleys, and of course their association with the Bentley name continued both during the 1930s and after World War 2.

Other exponents of the semi-Weymann system were Avon, Freestone & Webb, Hoyal, Gurney Nutting, and Martin Walter. Nevertheless, the significance of the semi-Weymann development is that it pointed the way to building flexible, coachbuilt bodies – in other words, bodies that were inherently flexible and yet which could still carry metal panelling.

Within a short time the French coachbuilder Vanvooren developed the new system further, using the new Silentbloc bushes to attach each "cell" of framework to the chassis. This became known as the "Silent Travel" system, which was eagerly adopted by a number of coachbuilders at the beginning of the 1930s.

The Silent Travel system had in fact been in use since 1929, by the Vanvooren coachbuilding company of Paris, but not initially under that name; they described such bodies as being constructed on "modified Weymann" principles, in that the separate plates were "hinged on Silentbloc bushes throughout". (The Silentbloc bush was one of the first examples of the newly-developed ability to bond rubber to steel; it consisted of two concentric bushes, with rubber in between to which each was bonded.)

When M Dasté, the owner of Vanvooren, finally launched his system, it was indeed based on the Silentbloc bush, both at framework joints and where the frame was mounted to the chassis. As with the "semi-Weymann" approach, the body frame was effectively three separate cells which could move relative to each other. The difference was that any flexing was taken up entirely at the Silentbloc bushes; thus each cell could be made totally rigid, and could be metal-panelled all over instead of having to be partially fabric-covered, with all the advantages (primarily cellulose finish) which that brought.

This was probably the most successful of the post-Weymann systems. It appeared to satisfy all the requirements – lightness, quietness and the finest coachbuilt appearance. Its period of popularity was too late for most vintage Bentleys, but there were a few exceptions, built by Vanden Plas on late-completion cars in 1931 and 1932.

It did not take the top London coachbuilders long to realise that the Bentley Three Litre was one of the chassis they should be targeting. This is a comparatively early example, chassis 279 from August 1923, and it bears Park Ward saloon bodywork.

A Gurney Nutting Three Litre saloon (chassis 405) from the same era makes an interesting comparison, its higher waist line contrasting with the more airy Park Ward saloon. No doubt this is partly due to Gurney Nutting having recently adopted the Weymann principle of construction – one of the first British coachbuilders to do so.

The Gurney Nutting saloon looks even more high-waisted in this three-quarter view.

This is the interior of the Gurney Nutting saloon, still in its original unrestored state. For the driver, getting in and out past the forest of levers was quite a test.

Here we have two early (1923) Three Litres which have seen better days. The first, a Freestone & Webb "fabric saloon" on chassis 164, must have been constructed to their own design since it predates their involvement with a Weymann licence.

The second is a Vanden Plas saloon on chassis 238, and when it was new was proudly given an "eggshell" finish. Note that Vanden Plas retained the vee-windscreen, whereas Freestone & Webb had already moved on to a flat design.

Here we have a very early example of the six-cylinder 6½ Litre model, with a Freestone & Webb saloon body dating from some time in 1924. This is the first experimental chassis, popularly known as "The Sun", and used as an illustration for the Bentley catalogue. The radiator still carries its disguise from when the car was used for secret testing.

The chassis of this Three Litre saloon has not been identified, but it probably dates from 1924. The coachwork is by London coachbuilders Harrison, who bodied nearly 200 vintage Bentley chassis.

The Vanden Plas Olympia Show car from 1924, on long-wheelbase Three Litre chassis 763. Finished in light grey and black, it had silver-plated interior fittings. The Vanden Plas style has already moved on, with a noticeably lower roof and a shallower vee to the windscreen.

It is hard to believe that this Vanden Plas Three Litre saloon also dates from 1924. The enormously tall glass-house must have been demanded by a more conservative customer who still insisted on wearing his top hat.

This Three Litre saloon, from about 1924, is an early example of Weymann construction from Freestone & Webb. These first Weymann efforts had a particularly squared-off appearance with an absence of compound curves. It was normal practice to apply the fabric only to the passenger compartment and the scuttle, as in this case.

This is an early Weymann saloon from H J Mulliner, on an unidentified Three Litre chassis but dated to December 1924. Already this firm have managed to introduce some curves to the lines of the car, which gives a significant improvement to its appearance.

The second six-cylinder experimental chassis, EX2, registration MH 1030. It was used extensively by W O Bentley for testing and was also used to test the 8 Litre engine. It was sold by H M Bentley in 1931, having been rebodied as a Vanden Plas tourer.

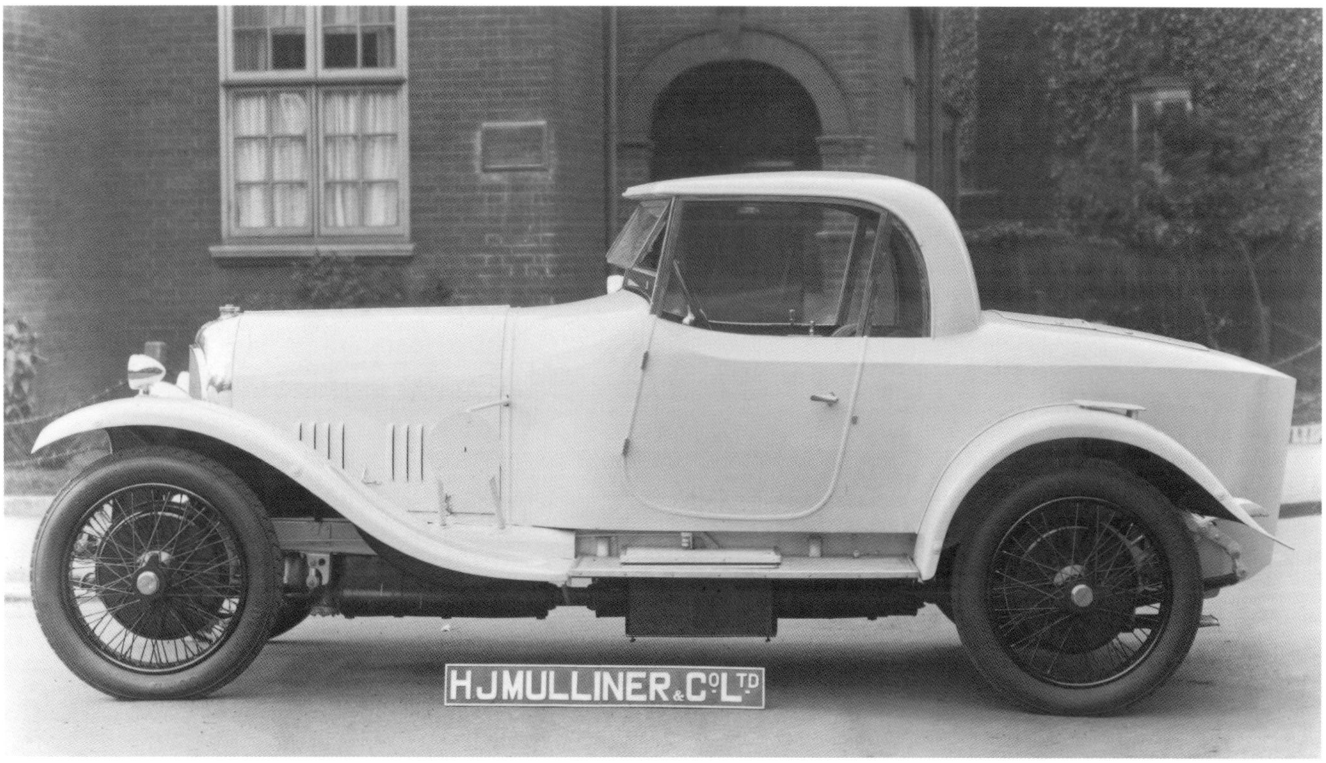

H J Mulliner could produce sporty-looking coachwork if required. This example, on an unknown Three Litre Speed Model chassis, dates from April 1926. It is listed as being built on Weymann principles, but this seems unlikely from the photograph.

A continental street scene proves that Bentleys were used for what they did best – high-speed touring, preferably abroad. This saloon, on 6½ Litre chassis WB2566, was built by the respected provincial coachbuilder Hamshaw of Leicester in mid-1926.

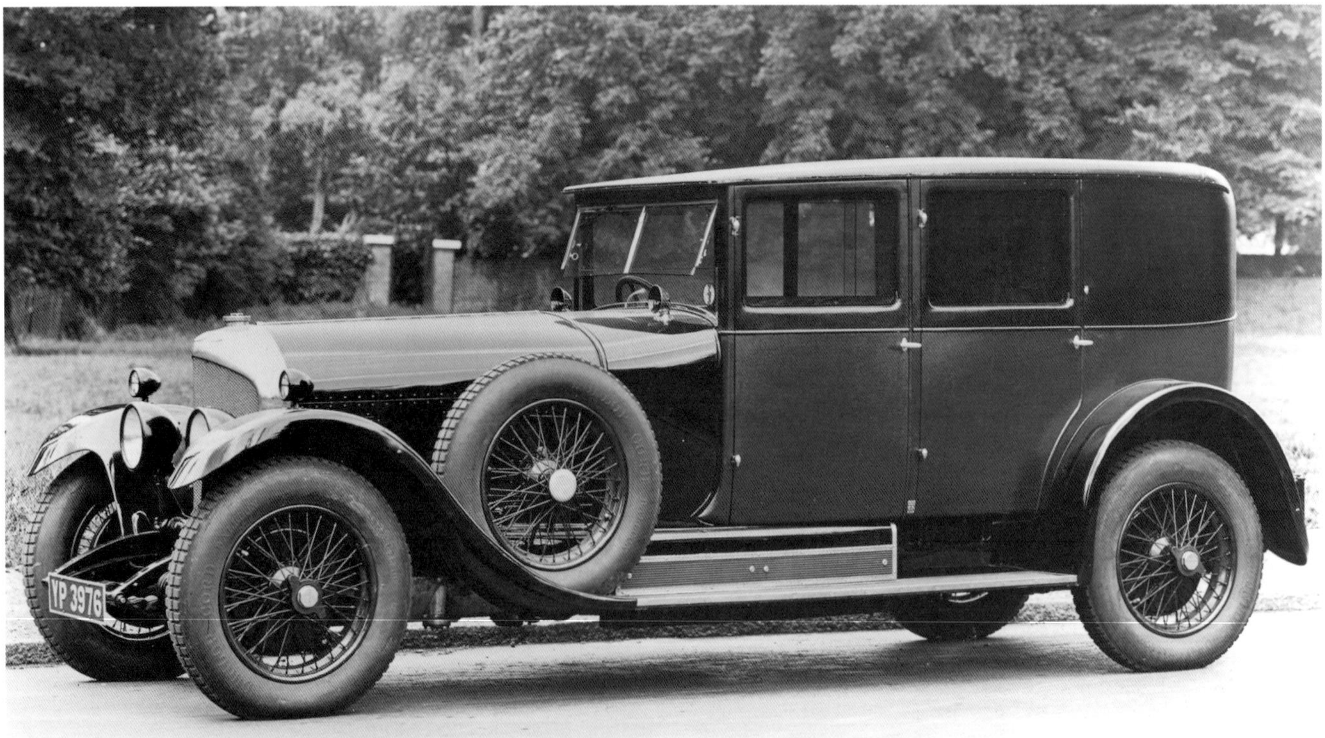

Here Gurney Nutting have used the longer bonnet of the 6½ Litre to good effect, blending it in with the stylish lines of the remainder of the car. This is chassis TB2530 from July 1926, and although it was listed as a landaulet it is clearly no such thing.

Another mid-1926 car is this Weymann saloon from Freestone & Webb, on chassis RT1543. Note the oval rear window. Although the car has clearly had a hard life, it still oozes character.

Yet another Weymann saloon from Freestone & Webb, this time on a later-1926 $6\frac{1}{2}$ Litre chassis, FW2609. The interest here is of course the designer's early – and quite successful – attempt at incorporating a luggage boot.

Weymann bodies were particularly suitable for the Speed Model Three Litre chassis because of their light weight. This is a Gurney Nutting "Speed Weymann", chassis LT1581, dating from November 1926.

It is quite astounding that coachwork of this design could be demanded by a customer as late as 1926. The open driver's compartment, and the luggage rails on the roof, date back to 1920, and indeed to pre-World War 1. This example, 6½ Litre chassis WK2657 by H J Mulliner, from November 1926, was listed as a landaulet, but it appears to be a limousine.

This 6½ Litre saloon, on chassis FW2607, is from the Norwich coachbuilders Howes & Sons. Its tall glasshouse and vee-windscreen somewhat belie its December 1926 date.

Vanden Plas's seven-passenger limousine on their Olympia Show stand in 1926 was fitted with interior heating and finished in "café-au-lait". This firm clung to vee-windscreens longer than most. The chassis is 6½ Litre FW2605.

This is the sumptuous interior of the same Vanden Plas 1926 Show car, with swivelling occasional seats and veneered panelling.

Another experimental chassis, Exp 4, was fitted with this Weymann saloon in about 1927. The coachbuilder is not known, but was probably Freestone & Webb. It is shown here in use by the Burgess family (Frederick Burgess was Bentley's chief designer). The typical fabric finish shows up well in this photograph. Note also the dummy hood-irons at the rear.

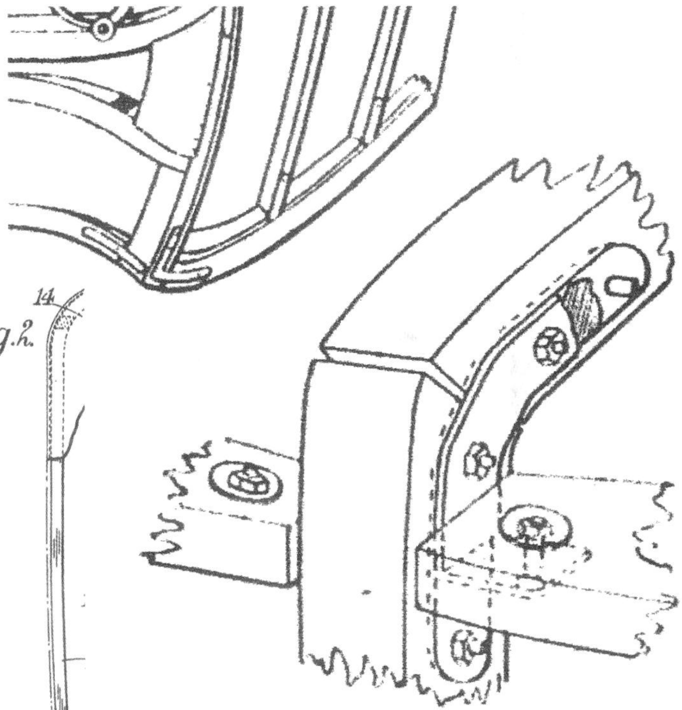

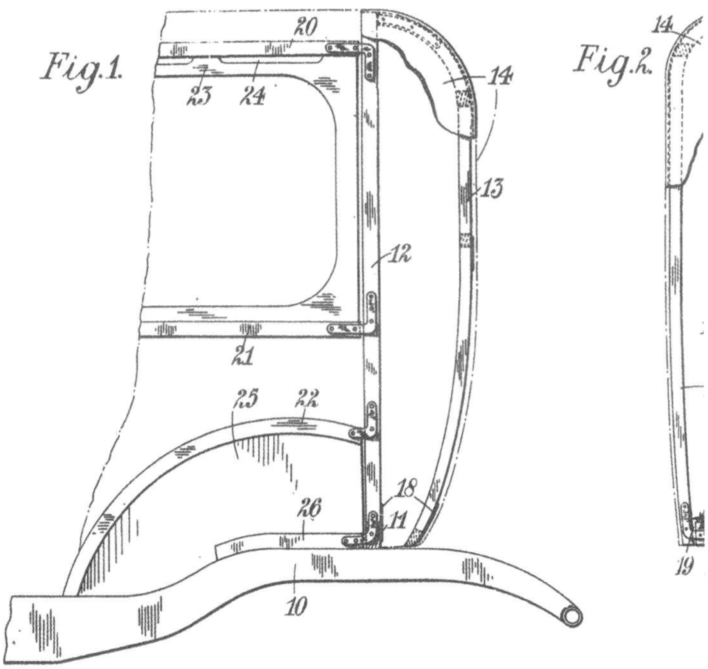

These two sketches – one from a patent application – illustrate the details of the Weymann method of constructing the wooden frame. Note that the joints are made by metal plates, with the wooden components held slightly apart so that they cannot squeak.

This is a Freestone & Webb saloon from early 1927, on 6½ Litre chassis TW2705. It is a graphic demonstration of what designers could produce when they were not constrained by the limitations of the Weymann system. Only the height of the body off the ground proclaims it as a 1920s rather than early 1930s style.

This Three Litre chassis also dates from 1927, but Freestone & Webb's Weymann saloon design has hardly moved forward in four years. The only nod to fashion is the pair of dummy hood-irons, a device which breaks up the large expanse of fabric on the rear quarter. Note also the "brougham" line to the front door, which allowed designers to use a near-parallel scuttle and thus avoid expensive panel-beating.

Gurney Nutting's Weymann saloon on Three Litre chassis AX1656 also dates from mid-1927, but is inherently more attractive with its multitude of curves, including the way in which the scuttle makes the transition from bonnet to passenger compartment.

A Gurney Nutting design on Three Litre Speed Model chassis AX1664 from mid-1927. What used to be an extended tail with dickey-seat on drophead coupés is now evolving into something more closely resembling a luggage-boot.

H J Mulliner produced this saloon design on Three Litre chassis ML1522 as late as September 1927, but one questions whether they were proud of the result. The tall windows are totally out of proportion with the height of the bonnet, and were probably there because of the customer's insistence.

Gurney Nutting built this 4½ Litre Weymann saloon, on chassis ST3013, in late 1927. Considering that it had lasted well over 20 years when this picture was taken, it survived very well. Note the glass louvres over the side-windows, an innovation at the time.

Right and below: This 1927 6 ½ Litre was originally a Park Ward coupé, body number 3055, but seen here clothed in a Martin Walter coupé, transplanted from Speed Six chassis number SB 2761. It shows a major step forward in the way the roof line has been lowered, probably by lowering the seats in the chassis. The bonnet line remains high, however, and this combination led to the "letter-box windscreen" style.

A most unusual piece of coachwork, built by Barker in late 1927. It is a 6½ Litre model, thought to be chassis KD2122. Alleged to be the Olympia Show car, and variously described as a limousine or sedanca de ville, it seems to fall into neither of these categories, and if anything might well be a landaulet. It shows the beginnings of streamline tendencies, with flared wings and float-type running-boards.

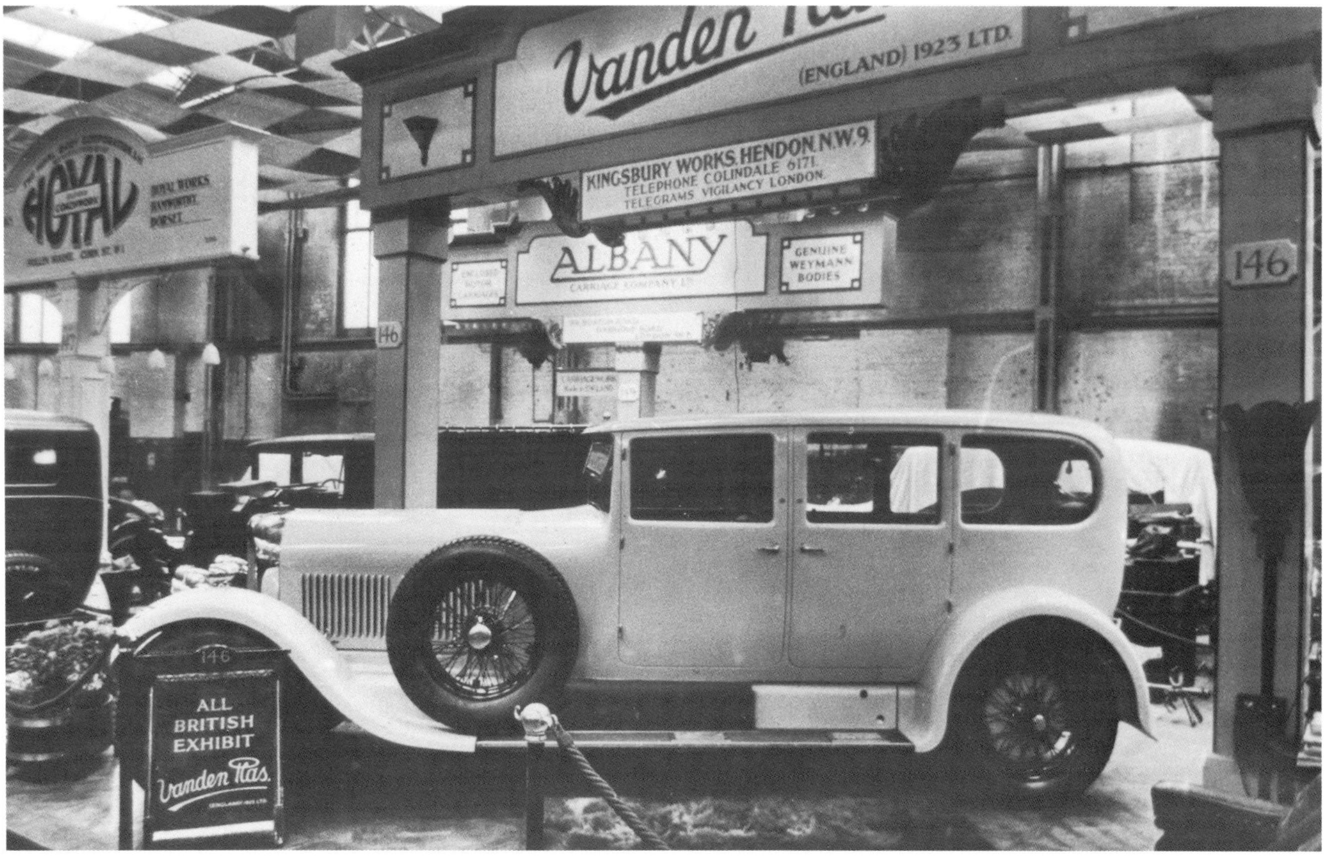

At the 1927 Olympia Show, Vanden Plas featured this vast limousine, of almost epic proportions, on the longest 6½ Litre chassis (KD2125). It is discernible that they, too, are beginning to lower their roof lines.

Barker's exhibit for the Scottish Show in December 1927, on 6½ Litre chassis PR2316. Even though the roof line is comparatively low, they have avoided shallow windows by dropping the waist line somewhat, and the whole appearance is made much more attractive as a result.

H J Mulliner built this 4½ Litre Weymann saloon (HF3190) in early 1928, but its peaked roof and ornate dummy hood-irons did it no favours. The wheel discs, not necessarily fitted by the coachbuilder, do not help lighten the overall effect.

The builder of this Weymann saloon on 4½ Litre chassis TX3249 from late 1928 is not known, but it could well have been H J Mulliner. The fashion is now for helmet wings and steps instead of running-boards, but note that the fitted luggage-trunk has also arrived.

Another Freestone & Webb Weymann saloon, on 4½ Litre chassis PM3257. Compared with Gurney Nutting, this coachbuilder preferred a higher waistline which made the windows shallower. In order to avoid the doors appearing over-deep, he has stopped them above the chassis and filled in with a valance.

Victor Broom were a well-known London coachbuilding firm during the 1920s, and they built this saloon on 6½ Litre chassis MD2470 in 1928. The car was eventually fitted with a P6 Perkins diesel engine and was last heard of in 1950.

The interior shot of the Victor Broom car shows the high standard of dashboard layout and controls. At the right-hand side, behind the gear-lever and handbrake, can be discerned the glow-plug switch for the diesel engine.

Weymann saloons with an attached luggage trunk were by now (1928) the standard product for upmarket saloons. Here are two views of a Gurney Nutting design on 4½ Litre chassis MF 3155, nicely restored and still going. Note that, in order to avoid the doors appearing too deep, the designer has raised the level of the running-boards to halfway up the chassis.

Later in1928, however, Gurney Nutting endowed this Speed Six chassis, WT2265, with a more sporting appearance by adopting cycle wings with no running-boards. The add-on luggage trunk has now become shaped to the rear of the car. This is the prototype Speed Six, used as a works demonstrator and road-tested in The Motor.

Above and right: In this Gurney Nutting example, 6½ Litre chassis FA2507, the designer has been forced by his desired wing shape to use low running-boards, and has filled in the gap below the doors with a chassis valance.

H J Mulliner joined in the Weymann saloon battle with this version on 4½ Litre chassis XR3345 of late 1928. Note the heavily peaked roof. The roof fabric appears to be of the new, glossy "tole souple" variety.

Freestone & Webb's Weymann 4½ Litre saloon has now followed the sporting route and adopted helmet front wings. However, the design has not gone the whole way, since it features a single-piece running-board rather than two individual steps below front and rear doors. The chassis number is not known, but it can be dated to January 1929.

Here the extra power of a Speed Six (chassis KF2381) is being put to useful purpose – though perhaps not one intended by the car's designer. The Weymann saloon is by Gurney Nutting, from early 1929, and the two-tone finish sets off its lines well.

The Victor Broom company make another appearance, with their own Weymann saloon on Speed Six chassis LB2328, also early 1929. There are numerous modern features about this design, including the sloping windscreen, glass window-louvres and built-in luggage trunk. Here the coachbuilder has chosen to use shorter doors, and to cover the chassis with a valance.

A Speed Six Weymann saloon, on chassis BA2582, bodied by the Bristol Aeroplane company. The leather fabric is particularly glossy in this shot, but it did not remain that way long enough for most owners, who were inevitably drawn towards cellulose finishes.

This Gurney Nutting effort from April 1929, which looks like a Weymann, was on 4½ Litre chassis MR3393. It was listed as a "saloon", but the fact that it has only two doors would tend to categorise it as more of a fixed-head coupé – indeed "faux cabriolet" because of the dummy pram-irons. It is another example of the different body styles gradually merging during the 1920s.

There was usually something "right" about the proportions of H J Mulliner saloons, and this is a good example. It is on 4½ Litre chassis NX3459, of early 1929, and is clearly of Weymann construction.

Here is another Gurney Nutting Speed Six design which, although designated as a saloon, could quite justifiably be called a fixed-head coupé – and indeed this is how we shall refer to this style from now on. It is on chassis LB2338 of mid-1929, and its louvred chassis-valance and twin spare wheels add to its sporting appearance.

At the 1929 Olympia Show Vanden Plas exhibited two Bentleys, one of which was this Speed Six, chassis KR 2689. It was built using the British Flexible system, devised and patented by the Harrison company. The finish was fawn fabric on the upper parts and maroon fabric on the lower, with the wings and bonnet in maroon cellulose and fawn wheels.

This is 4½ Litre, chassis PL3484. with a Vanden Plas saloon body which had seen a bit of service. After they had left vee-windscreens behind, this firm's cars were as modern-looking as the best.

The Speed Six chassis, in particular, inspired coachbuilders to design more sporting bodywork. This one, FR2631 of mid-1929, has been bodied by Freestone & Webb in two-door form, and the sporting characteristics are emphasised by the helmet wings and vestigial running-boards. Note how the width of the door allows it to be taken down to chassis level without appearing too tall and narrow.

This style of Weymann saloon from Freestone & Webb, known as the Standard Six, is seen here on chassis WT2267 of late 1928. It is a conventional design, retaining running-boards and chassis valances, and the dummy hood-irons remain the only slight extravagance.

Here and on the following pages we have a set of photos of another 1928 car, this time 6½ Litre chassis FA2504 bearing Gurney Nutting limousine coachwork. The car is totally original but has been restored to a high standard.

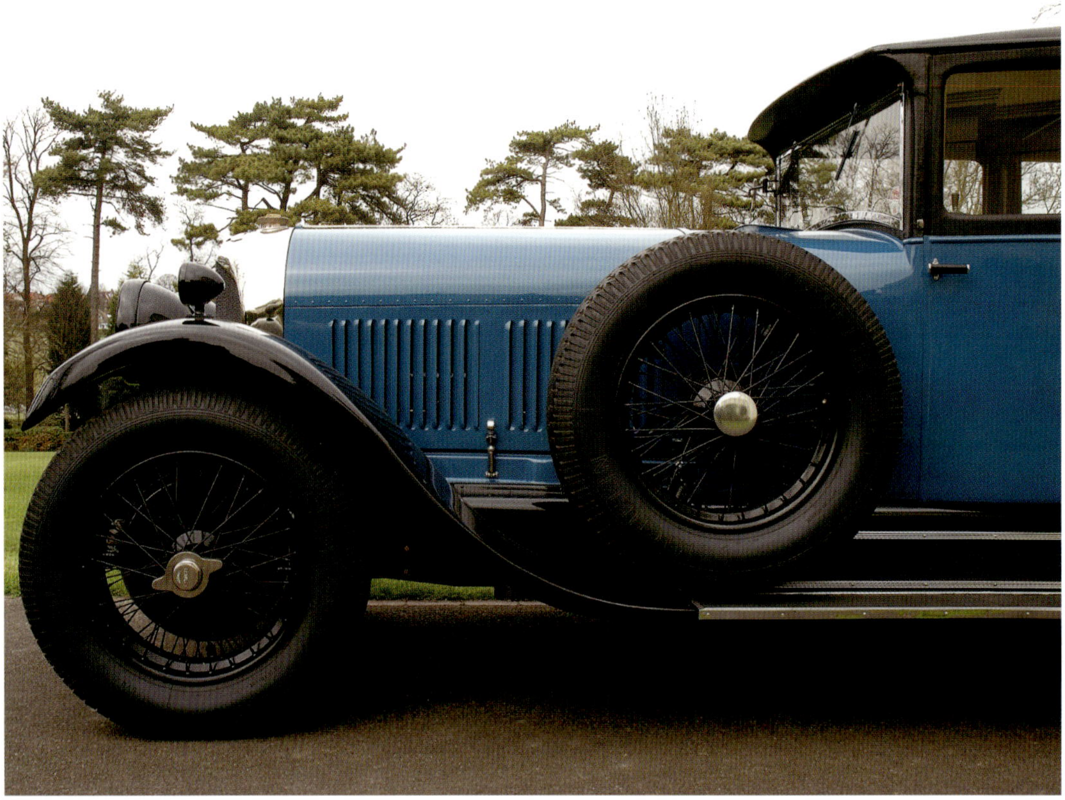

A peaked roof was regarded as an essential feature for a saloon or limousine at this period, before aerodynamic considerations led to it being abandoned.

Vee- and three-panel windscreens have now been dropped in place of single-piece versions, usually – as here – opening by being hinged from the top.

The particular interest in this body is that it is of "semi-Weymann" or "panelled Weymann" construction, wherein the roof and rear quarters are fabric-covered while the lower portion is of metal panels.

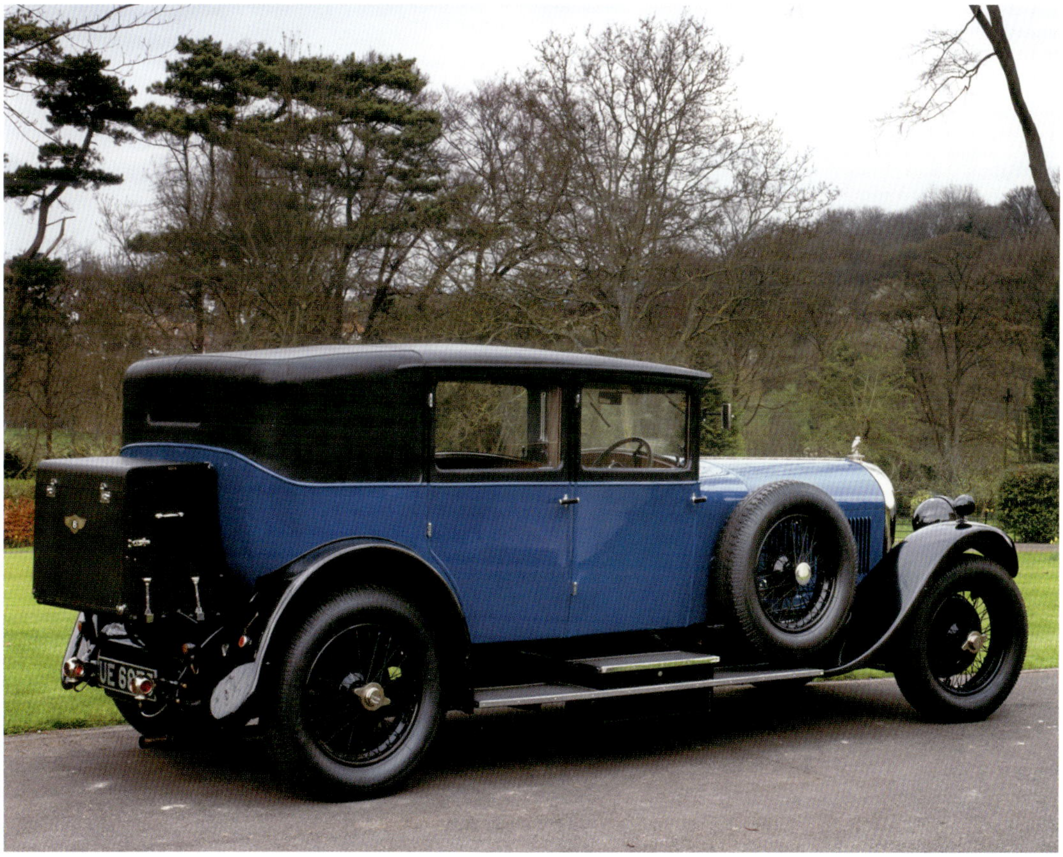

The result more closely resembles a conventional "coachbuilt" body rather than a standard Weymann one – particularly as the metal panels can be given the gloss finish which comes with cellulose paint.

The interior is luxurious, if a little dark. It was difficult with the Weymann roof construction to provide windows in the rear quarters.

Occasional seats swing out of the division. Note the winding handle for raising and lowering the glass portion of the division.

Fitted cocktail cabinets were not unusual in coachwork of this quality.

The chauffeur could cover the rear window with a blind at night if he was dazzled by the lights of a following car.

The built-in luggage trunk was on its way but had not quite arrived. In theory it could be removed "for town work". It was as capacious as the steamer trunks which had previously been used, and probably more practical to use.

Exiting via the driver's door was particularly difficult, because of the forest of levers in the way.

Our next colour collection features a Speed Six from 1929, chassis FR2644 with a Freestone & Webb four-door Weymann saloon body. The car has been restored only where necessary, and otherwise retains many features which are absolutely original.

A side view immediately reveals one feature which is most unusual for a Weymann body – a "light" (ie window) in the rear quarter.

True to the fashion of the time, the front wings are of the cycle type. They provide more room for the spare wheel, but give the designer a problem in finishing the running-boards.

There is ample space in the saloon's rear compartment, but unlike with limousines or landaulets there are no occasional seats.

Since there is no division, the front seats can be made individually adjustable. The standard of trim is equal to that in the rear compartment – essential in an "owner-driver" car.

By this period running-boards were sited low down. Rather than use a decorative chassis valance, the designer has made the doors extra deep so that they extend downwards to the running-boards.

There are two underfloor lockers each side, filling the space between body and chassis.

Many designers solved the cycle wing problem by using a step instead of a running-board. Here, however, Freestone & Webb used a horizontal running-board and finished it off neatly behind the spare wheel.

The peaked roof was still in fashion in 1929, but about to disappear.

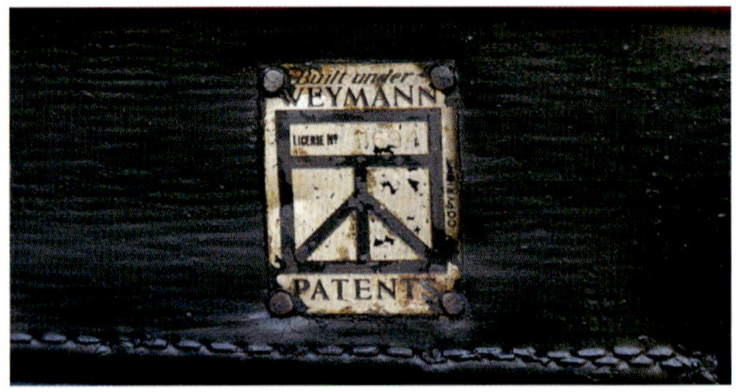

One of these plates went into every body built under a Weymann licence.

Above: The previously separate luggage trunk has started to become an integral part of the design.

A fold-down grid allows for extra luggage beyond the capacity of the trunk.

A Gurney Nutting Weymann saloon (KR2699) is shown here leading the 1929 Lord Mayor's Show in London. Note how this coachbuilder is developing a quite different form of front wing, pointed at the forward edge and with a swage line running down the centre.

Yet another Weymann saloon from Gurney Nutting, this time on the long standard chassis (KR2690). By this time, late 1929, glass window-louvres were becoming a comparatively common feature.

H J Mulliner's approach to the design of a Weymann saloon on the Speed Six chassis (BA2583) at the same time (late 1929), has the company's characteristic roof sloping up towards the rear, but is also slightly daring in going to helmet wings at the front. Note the bumpers front and rear, by no means a common feature.

Another H J Mulliner saloon – looking like a Weymann again – on 4½ Litre chassis PB3526, shows them experimenting with a sloping windscreen at last. This car dates from December 1929.

There were three different coachbuilders during the 1920s bearing the name "Mulliner"; Arthur Mulliner of Northampton were a well-regarded provincial firm. This is thought to be their exhibit at the 1929 Scottish Show, 4½ Litre chassis PB3529. It is bang up to date, with helmet wings, louvred chassis valances, glass window-louvres and, it would appear, luggage accommodation in the tail.

The high standard of trim can be seen from the interior shot. At the time this design would have been described as a "sportsman's coupé", a style which was extremely popular for a short period.

Victor Broom built this Speed Six saloon (chassis KR2698) in December 1929, and gave it a slightly more sporting appearance by sloping the windscreen backwards. The car was on the firm's stand at the 1929 Olympia Show; here it is apparently performing at the Brighton Speed Trials.

Maythorn were a highly-regarded provincial coachbuilder located at Biggleswade in Bedfordshire, who unfortunately went out of business in 1931. The Weymann fixed-head coupé shown here dates from the end of 1929 and was built on 4½ Litre chassis XF3511.

If anything marks out a Park Ward style around this period it is the slightly bulbous rear quarter, as shown in this 6½ Litre limousine from around 1930. It would seem that the construction is "semi-Weymann", since the lower panels appear to be metal rather than fabric.

An H J Mulliner Speed Six fixed-head coupé from early 1930 uses its long bonnet, low roof and continuous waistline to give an impression of power and speed, an effect successfully achieved here. The chassis is NH2735.

Another Speed Six fixed-head coupé, this time from the Folkestone firm of Martin Walter. Here the continuous waistline is again featured, and falls off distinctly towards the tail, a style which would become common during the 1930s. The chassis is SB2761.

Here we have one of the minority of Weymann bodies which were built by the Weymann company themselves. It is on 4½ Litre chassis AD3654, and while the design has all the necessary up-to-date features, its excessively high roof line has the unfortunate effect of making the car look rather small.

A few Bentley chassis were bodied abroad. This one, on Speed Six chassis HM2854 dating from mid-1930, was bodied as a limousine by Schutte of the United States.

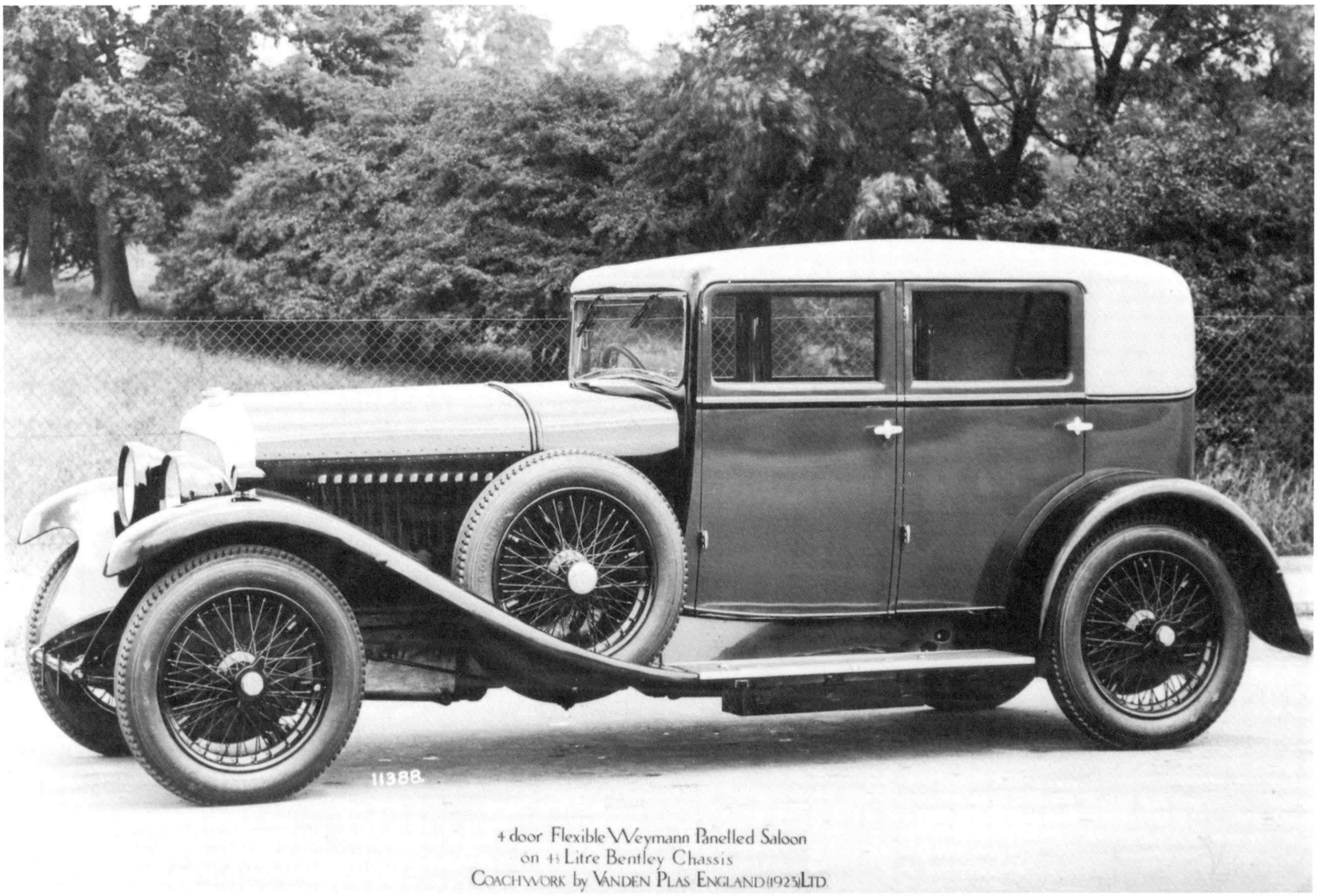

This is a Vanden Plas 4½ Litre saloon, constructed in the semi-Weymann or "flexible Weymann panelled" method. It is on chassis FS3601, and was finished in a combination of blue and black. It dates from July 1930.

This Speed Six two-door saloon, chassis HM2861, was bodied by the dashing Corsica Coachworks in late 1930. Corsica's reputation was for fulfilling clients' wishes direct from sketches rather than going through the boring process of detailed drawings.

Here we have the second Eight Litre chassis produced, said to be W O's personal car. Chassis number is YF5002 dating from October 1930, and the coachwork is a Weymann saloon by H J Mulliner. The sheer size of the car is most impressive.

Even by late 1930 not all saloons were given a luggage-trunk, as shown by this Freestone & Webb 4½ Litre on chassis FS3614. It appears to be of orthodox Weymann construction, at a time when that method was rapidly going out of favour.

By contrast to the previous photograph, this H J Mulliner Speed Six fixed-head coupé (chassis LR2778), from the same period (late 1930), appears to be of semi-Weymann construction and has much more up-to-date lines, even hinting at what was to come in the early 1930s.

Gurney Nutting's treatment of a fixed-head coupé on a Speed Six chassis, from early 1931, is even more advanced. There is a forward slope to the front of the door, matching the backward slope of the windscreen. This chassis is believed to be HM2864.

Above and top right: Here are two views of another huge Eight Litre car, chassis YF5022 from early 1931, bodied by Park Ward. Their description of the style is "limousine de ville", but there is no sign that one can slide back the whole canopy from the driver's compartment. There is no suggestion of this car demeaning itself by carrying luggage; that was a job for the railway carrier or the second car.

This Eight Litre saloon was bodied by Freestone & Webb in early 1931, on chassis YF5025. It is wholly up to date, with a falling waistline and an integrated luggage compartment. Note that cycle wings are still deemed essential.

GN 4110

Gurney Nutting show further progress with their fixed-head coupé designs. This is Eight Litre chassis YR5088 from April 1931, and compared with the last Speed Six we saw (page 77) – only a few months earlier – this version shows a more confident treatment of the rear wings and luggage-trunk. The spare wheel is a problem. however.

Yet another Eight Litre saloon – but what a revelation! Freestone & Webb bodied chassis YR5091 in the spring of 1931, and in one move advanced saloon design by several years. The unanswered question is the manner of its construction, since it appears to be neither Weymann nor semi-Weymann but built by orthodox panelled-frame methods.

In this case we do know the method Vanden Plas used when they built a saloon on an Eight Litre chassis. This is one of three built during 1931 using their so-called "Silentbloc" system, which they had borrowed from Vanvooren of France and which eventually became known as Silent Travel. For some reason they have reverted to the old-fashioned "brougham door" shape, but in other respects the design is up to the minute, particularly with its sloping windscreen, front wings wrapping round the front of the wheel and faired-in sidelights.

When the Four-Litre arrived it generated designs which were the equal of those on the Eight Litre – unsurprisingly, since the two chassis were virtually identical. This is a semi-Weymann saloon by H J Mulliner on chassis VF4004 from May 1931, and was the personal property of Woolf Barnato. Note the shiny "tole souple" fabric on the roof and rear quarter, and also the waist moulding along the length of the car. The luggage boot has now become wholly integrated into the design.

Here we see a more formal limousine treatment from Freestone & Webb, on Eight Litre chassis VF5010. This, too, dates from May 1931, and was also Barnato's own property. It is being ceremonially "towed" back to his home after his wedding.

Two shots (above and opposite) of an even more spectacular limousine from Freestone & Webb, who have taken "long and low" to new extremes. It is on Eight Litre chassis VM5032 of June 1931. The frontal view, taken at a different time when the car was in a darker colour, is equally impressive, and shows how waist mouldings and wing swage-lines were becoming normal features.

Once again we have to decide whether this style is a two-door saloon or a fixed-head coupé. Either way, when Freestone & Webb designed it for Eight Litre chassis YF5021, they must have found a way of lowering the seats even more than usual in order to achieve such a low roof or perhaps headroom was sacrified for fashion. The date is mid-1931.

The Eight Litre chassis clearly inspired Freestone & Webb to ever new heights. This saloon, on chassis YR5089 from September 1931, is even more advanced than their work earlier in the year. The domed wings faired in to the running-boards, and the waist moulding expanded into a swage-line on the rear door, would have been innovative three or four years later.

H J Mulliner somehow managed to make Four Litre chassis VF4018 (from September 1931) look smaller than it was when they designed this fixed-head coupé body. The triangular glazed panel in front of the dummy hood-irons is an unusual feature.

This is Four Litre chassis VF4097, one of those completed in 1932 well after the Rolls-Royce takeover. The saloon body is by Gurney Nutting, and features a slightly ungainly version of the "brougham" shape to the front door.

Another 1932 completion, this is one of the last Eight Litre chassis, YX5110. Its H J Mulliner saloon body shows clear evidence of being a 1930s design with its integral luggage boot and scalloped front wings.

Chapter Two

Cabriolets, Drophead Coupés and Landaulets

One important difference between carriage-building and motor bodywork manufacture was in its frequency of purchase. If we ignore commercial applications such as farm-carts, drays, hansom cabs and so on, the life of a carriage built for social purposes was very much longer than that of a car – even of a car in motoring's earliest days. No doubt this was partly a result of the greatly increased mileages of which motorcars were capable, leading to them being replaced of necessity after a relatively short time. On the other hand there was also from the beginning an element of novelty about having a new car, which led to its owner being tempted to replace it long before it was technically necessary.

It was this relative infrequency of purchase which led to the practice of carriage-builders producing only bespoke designs. Whereas commercial carts or drays could be built and sold to a relatively standardised design, there was little if any advantage in trying to persuade a client for a town carriage to have something that was "off the shelf". On the contrary, there was everything to be said for a carriage-builder enhancing his reputation by creating new designs each time. Not only did a unique design give the client all the personal features which he happened to prefer, but it marked him out as a man of means and discrimination. When the first motorcars arrived, therefore, both builder and client were in a frame of mind which assumed that an individual body design was the normal way of doing things.

Another relic of horse-drawn practice, particularly amongst the British landed gentry, was a love of travelling in the open air. While this was a matter of necessity when actually riding a horse, it was a deliberate choice where carriages were concerned. Landaus, victorias and many other forms of carriage were designed to be used more with their hoods down than otherwise. We can guess at the reasons for the popularity of the open carriage – probably a combination of the desire to be seen and to make an impression in town, together with a perception of its benefit to health in the country. Whatever the motivation, this preference was naturally carried over to motorcar bodies, even after closed versions became widely available.

These two factors – the desire to commission one's own unique design, and a love of the open air – combined in the early days of motoring to ensure that open coachwork was both more varied and more up-to-date in its styling. Added to this was the realisation that open bodies were always lighter than their closed counterparts, and therefore gave the car better performance. All these influences can still be discerned in the open bodywork of the 1920s, and together they ensure that its styling is an endless source of fascination.

When we consider open bodywork there are numerous coachbuilders' descriptions jostling for attention. It will be helpful if we group them together – first cabriolets with landaulets, and then tourers (including sports models) with all-weathers. The reasoning is that the first two are (or were at the time) more formal styles, while the tourer and sports were clearly less so. In between is the all-weather, which originally was a kind of upmarket tourer but which gradually disappeared, squeezed between cabriolets and tourers.

Let us start by defining drophead coupés, cabriolets

and landaulets. The cabriolet, as it existed at the start of the 1920s, was a drophead body with a division, and often without even having "enclosed drive". After a short time the requirement for the division was dropped, and the style – sometimes known as a "saloon cabriolet" – became virtually identical to an all-weather. If there was a distinction, it was the implication that a cabriolet had only two doors whereas one would expect an all-weather to have four. In two-door form a cabriolet therefore became synonymous with a drophead coupé. Its folding head normally extended over the front seats as well as the rear ones (if indeed there was a second row of seats), but did not extend far enough back to cover the dickey-seat where there was one.

A landaulet, on the other hand, was a cross between a limousine and a cabriolet. The forward part of the roof was fixed, while the rear portion was a folding head which could be let down to place the back-seat passengers in the open air. Once again, at the start of the 1920s it would almost certainly have had a division between the rear and front compartments. If this feature was omitted the style strictly speaking became a saloon landaulet, and as time went on this became the norm.

The early popularity of the landaulet seems to have been intimately bound up with the question of luggage. Many motorists, still in a horse-carriage mode of thinking, preferred to keep their luggage on the floor in front of the back-seat passengers. This had the advantage, in a closed car, of keeping it dry as well. Alternatively one could strap it to the running-board, and this was often the only place in an open car. Given this type of usage, one can see why running-boards were made so substantial in those days. A luggage-grid at the back was another solution, and indeed appeared quite early on in the first decade of the century. Not everyone approved of this solution, however, as the addition of so much weight at the rear extremity was thought to increase the risk of skidding. Best of all for many, though, was to be able to throw one's bags and cases on to the roof – again, just as people used to do with horse-drawn coaches.

It seems clear that the landaulet style was favoured at least in part because of this feature. One could open the greater part of the "saloon" to the elements, and yet have a strong front portion of the roof which would withstand the weight of baggage. *The Autocar* magazine, arguing in an early editorial that the landaulet was "the covered motor car of the future", became almost poetic: "When it is closed the back part of the car is as snug as the very snuggest brougham, and when fully opened as free as any uncovered car". They then rather spoiled their case by conceding that these advantages applied only to the rear seats, and that work was needed to extend them to the front ones as well. In these and other writings of the time one can see designers groping their way towards what became the cabriolet, but that could only come about once it became accepted that the roof was not the place for luggage.

One might pinpoint the moment when the cabriolet was born as being the 1906 Olympia Show. Hamshaw brought out a so-called landaulet which was so different from anything before that it had a motoring journalist groping for words. "The usual leather hood extends to the driver's screen, the front portion folds back flat against the front frame of the body, then the section[s] of the hood between the front supports and the rear door support fold up one upon the other, the whole lot falling back neatly on to the top of the back seats, thus leaving a completely open car for ordinary use. Though the whole of the top part is collapsable [sic], we are assured that the method of construction avoids all possibility of draughts, and affords as warm and comfortable an interior as the more usual landaulet."

By the start of the 1920s the cabriolet had firmly established itself, and its adherents were convinced of its superiority over the landaulet since it could be opened completely, whereas on a landaulet the side-pillars and the front part of the roof were always in position. In either case the coachwork was finished to a high standard, and since owners of such cars usually employed a chauffeur the front (driver's) compartment was still open to the elements. In such cars the hood would always be made of leather. As a writer in *The Autocar* put it (1921), "Neither a coupé nor an all-weather body will give continued satisfaction if the head be covered with imitation leather in place of the real thing. Exposure to the weather, and especially to sunlight, in addition to the close folding of the material when the head is thrown back, soon result in the surface of the covering developing innumerable cracks and eventually leaking badly. But no well-made head of either type has other than real leather covering."

There was one area above all where both the cabriolet and the landaulet were at a disadvantage – unless the latter still boasted the old-fashioned "roof rail". This was their ability to carry luggage, something to which – as we have seen – the designers of closed cars were paying increasing attention, with separate luggage trunks arriving by 1923 or 1924. The best that the cabriolet or landaulet could offer was a fold-down luggage-grid. However another solution was at hand, in the form of the drophead coupé. This style offered an attractive combination of open-air motoring for two, three or even four people, with three squeezed across the front seat and the fourth in an occasional seat in the tail, known to British coachbuilders as a "dickey seat" (and in some other countries as the "mother-in-law seat"). A flush-fitting lid covered the seat when it was not in use, and it did not take a feat of imagination to realise that the compartment so formed, which often contained the tool-kit, could also carry luggage.

To those who could afford such a car in those days, there was one increasingly important item of luggage: a set of golf clubs. Even when there was a luggage-boot, it was nowhere near wide enough to swallow so long a load, and designers came up with ingenious ways round the problem. The most popular solution was to provide a separate compartment, with its own door in the side panel, running across the width of the car behind the rear axle line. Another approach was that taken by William Arnold, the Manchester coachbuilder, who installed "receptacles" for golf-clubs on the running-boards of one car in 1921.

From this point on the two concepts, cabriolet and drophead coupé, rapidly became indistinguishable one from the other. It was only a matter of time before the latter's dickey-seat passenger was "covered in" by the hood – another way of saying that there were two rows of seats. At the same time the cabriolet gave up any claim to a division between front and rear compartment, making two-door versions feasible. The standard of fittings and trimming in such designs was in many ways as high as in closed cars, and indeed this was the main feature which distinguished them from tourers or two-door sports models.

During the 1920s designers continued to search for the Englishman's ideal body style, one which would assure him of total protection from wet and cold and yet permit him to enjoy the sun when it arrived. Their solutions often resulted in a halfway house, somewhere between the cabriolet and the saloon. Indeed there was a movement at one point to reserve the cabriolet description for this style only, but it did not receive sufficient support. The sunshine roof was of course one manifestation of this trend, but the finished result was still demonstrably a saloon. Less easy to define was the style which kept the doors, windows and (usually) cant-rails of the saloon, but did away with the roof and rear window. Best known of these designs was the Tickford (introduced in 1925 by the coachbuilder Salmons of Newport Pagnell), in which the folding roof mechanism was operated through a train of gears by a winding handle inserted in the car's rear quarter. Another design, by Alexander of Glasgow, used a chain and sprocket system. Salmons and Alexander called this style an "all-weather saloon", but other similar designs were often described as "cabriolets".

By the middle of the decade it was becoming clear that the drophead coupé was becoming favoured by owners who wanted to retain a degree of creature comfort which hard-nosed sportsmen would despise. In other words they liked some open air but not too much. Witness this description, from *The Autocar* magazine, of an exhibit on the 1925 Olympia Show stand of H J Mulliner: "Mounted on a 15.9 h.p. three-litre Bentley chassis, the two-seater coupé named 'Simplex' succeeds admirably in striking the sporting note without sacrificing comfort and even luxury. Finished in cream with wheels and leather upholstery to the adjustable armchair seats, of bright red, it is fitted with a sloping V-fronted screen, and, when open, the head disappears entirely, leaving a perfectly clean top line, despite the fact that a double dickey seat is provided." It is interesting to note that the previous year this same coachbuilder had shown an apparently very similar car, but had then described it as "a two-seater three-quarter Simplex cabriolet body with a two-seater dickey and a sliding front seat." Comfort still prevailed over any sporting pretensions: "The interior finish is antique brown leather, the outside paintwork is of 'ciel' colour, with black top and wings, a fascinating combination."

On the other hand the limitations of the landaulet style, with its lack of upward vision ahead of the passengers, were becoming apparent. Their numbers at Motor Shows gradually declined, although those that did appear were still built to the highest standards. "The [Gurney Nutting] Bentley saloon-landaulet, finished in Argyll blue, has auxiliary flush seats to the interior rear portion, with foot cushions and loose cushions for the back seats. It is upholstered in French fancy cloth, and the finish throughout is high class", said *The Autocar* in 1924. The following year William Arnold attracted attention with their Bentley "Arnaulet" (landaulet), if only because of its gaudy paintwork. "This body has only four side windows, those at the rear being exceptionally wide; folding adjustable front seats are fitted, and the panelled doors contain lock-up tool cabinets. The colour scheme of the Bentley is arresting to the eye, being compounded of primrose and mauve."

The argument still raged, of course, as to whether open bodywork of any description was worthwhile. As a provocative article in *The Motor* in 1926 put it: "Great Britain is famed for its die-hards. These sturdy individuals insist that they adore fresh air and love bright sunshine. They shut their eyes to the fact that the number of days in the year on which the sun shines brightly and warmly are very few. In any case, they will argue, one day in an open car in fine weather is worth a month in a stuffy saloon. Still, even the most confirmed open-car enthusiast will admit that for a long main-road journey the closed car possesses every advantage. A shower of rain is encountered and the windows are immediately closed without trouble, without slackening speed. A halt for lunch or dinner is made and the windows are closed and the doors locked, leaving coats, rugs and luggage safe in the car while it is parked. There is none of the concealing belongings beneath rugs and cushions that has to be resorted to if an open car is left unattended."

During the 1920s it gradually became evident that the cabriolet was the style of choice for those buyers who were interested in making a fashion statement. This led to the strange device whereby cars were made to look as if they were built in this style, even though their roofs were fixed. Nowadays we would describe such a car as a "fixed-head coupé", but originally they were known by the French title of "faux cabriolet" ('faux' meaning 'false'). Numerous devices were used to maintain this fiction, including covering the roof in fabric, which sat well with the "semi-Weymann" style later in the decade. However an early manifestation of the fashion was to add dummy hood-irons on the outside of the rear quarters. External hood-irons were themselves a comparative novelty, dating from around 1923, and the first "false" versions appeared less than three years later.

Once cabriolets had begun to move upmarket, they did so with relish. At the 1928 Olympia Show, for example, Victor Broom's exhibit was described thus: "Very attractive is the saxe-blue-and-cream cellulose-finished coupé on a 4½ Litre Bentley. The silk-lined leather head opens, the head lining matching the saxe-blue leather upholstery." And by 1930 two more examples show the direction in which these open styles were moving, firstly from Thrupp & Maberly: "A sports coupé on the new Eight-Litre Bentley chassis is really an open two-seater and coupé in one, as the head of the coupé when down is completely concealed beneath the rear decking. A large tail provides ample luggage accommodation, and other features are the raked screen, the helmet-type wings, and the general low build. The colour scheme is of black and a delicate shade of pastel blue. The interior woodwork is of quartered and veneered burr walnut, and all bright parts are chromium plated. The head is trimmed with black mohair piped with blue leather".

And the second example, from Gurney Nutting, is of the "de ville", the least sporting type of open car: "Also on an Eight Litre Bentley chassis is shown a coachbuilt sedanca de ville which is finished in birch grey with a black top. Grey cloth upholstery is used for the rear compartment, in which occasional seats are mounted, while the front seats are in black leather. The lines are enhanced by a chromium-plated deep beading carried right through from the radiator, and by semi-sporting-type wings."

Drophead coupés, just as much as closed cars, suffered from the late-1920s fashion for lower roof-lines. This stemmed from the streamlining craze, just starting at this period, which, when combined with longer bonnets, produced an impression of power and speed. Unfortunately the poor passengers had not at that point been lowered in sympathy, a point which *The Automobile Engineer* took up with some force (November 1926). Referring to the need for passengers to adopt "a most uncomfortable crouching attitude" when entering such cars, it went on: "Such disabilities could be much reduced by lowering the floor-boards inside the car. Floorboards are often raised appreciably above the frame level, and the frame itself is frequently a good deal higher than it need be. The craze for frame members straight in elevation has passed with the abandonment by many firms of quarter-elliptic front springs. The frame contour necessary for a lower floorboard position should not, therefore, be difficult to attain... It might be possible to arrange footwells also. In this way the feet of passengers would rest at a suitable and comfortable angle instead of in grotesque positions suggestive, in appearance and comfort, of partial dislocation."

The magazine showed great foresight in airing these two subjects. During the following year both "double-dropped" chassis and rear footwells began to be seen – an example of chassis manufacturers at last taking heed of the coachbuilder's needs. Unfortunately the same could not be said for another request in the same editorial – the return of the running-board ("their usefulness as carrying space for small luggage, their mudguarding action, and their finished appearance need no comment"). They had been deleted in favour of small steps and cycle wings, a fashion which would continue for several years.

One type of semi-open car which enjoyed something of a return to favour in the late 1920s was the "de ville" style, variously named sedanca de ville or cabriolet de ville. Quite why this should be, apart from some strange form of snobbery, is hard to fathom. *The Autocar*, reviewing coachwork trends in 1929, were equally baffled. "There is a preference for enclosed-drive cars among those who favour the town carriage type of vehicle, and there is really no reason why the occupants of the front seat should not have the complete protection from wind and rain afforded by properly constructed windows. The only possible objection that can be advanced against a window on the driver's side is that it may make signalling difficult, but as specially constructed windows to allow easy signalling are now employed, even this objection does not hold good."

This is an early Three Litre, and although its chassis number is not known its registration dates it at 1922. With the hood down it is not the prettiest of cars, but with the strange hood arrangement seen in the picture below it must be one of the ugliest drophead coupés of all time.

The double-hood feature may well have been the first owner's own design, and he was so proud of it that he photographed the brand-new car in front of his stately home. We do not know who the coachbuilder was

This 1923 Three Litre drophead by Penman of Dumfries is a lighter and more satisfying design. In particular, because of its flat windscreen, it does away with the extraordinary structure on top of the screen rail. Like all dropheads of its time, it appears to have a dickey-seat.

An early chassis (191), this is the landaulet style which was so popular before and just after World War 1 before it rapidly went out of fashion. It is built on the long-wheelbase chassis to give maximum legroom in the rear compartment.

Rippon of Huddersfield were one of the very highest-class provincial coachbuilders, whose work would stand comparison with the very best from London. With its hood down, this early (no front brakes) chassis shows distinct flair with its polished bonnet and swept front wings. With hood erected, however, the whole effect is spoilt, and there is a distinct horse-and-carriage flavour about the line of the hood and rear quarter.

In this 1925 design, H J Mulliner showed two advanced ideas for the time – a concealed hood and a sloping, flat windscreen. The attractive design demonstrates the extra freedom designers enjoyed when working with metal-panelled construction methods rather than Weymann.

Not to be outdone, Gurney Nutting also used a sloping windscreen together with a bold, flared front wing on their design of the same year, on Three Litre chassis 1222. On this occasion the design did not extend to a concealed head.

Once the 6½ Litre extended chassis had arrived, coachbuilders had much more freedom to produce long, powerful-looking designs. An unusual feature here is the lack of louvres in the bonnet; there appear to be ventilating doors instead. Note the leather chassis valance.

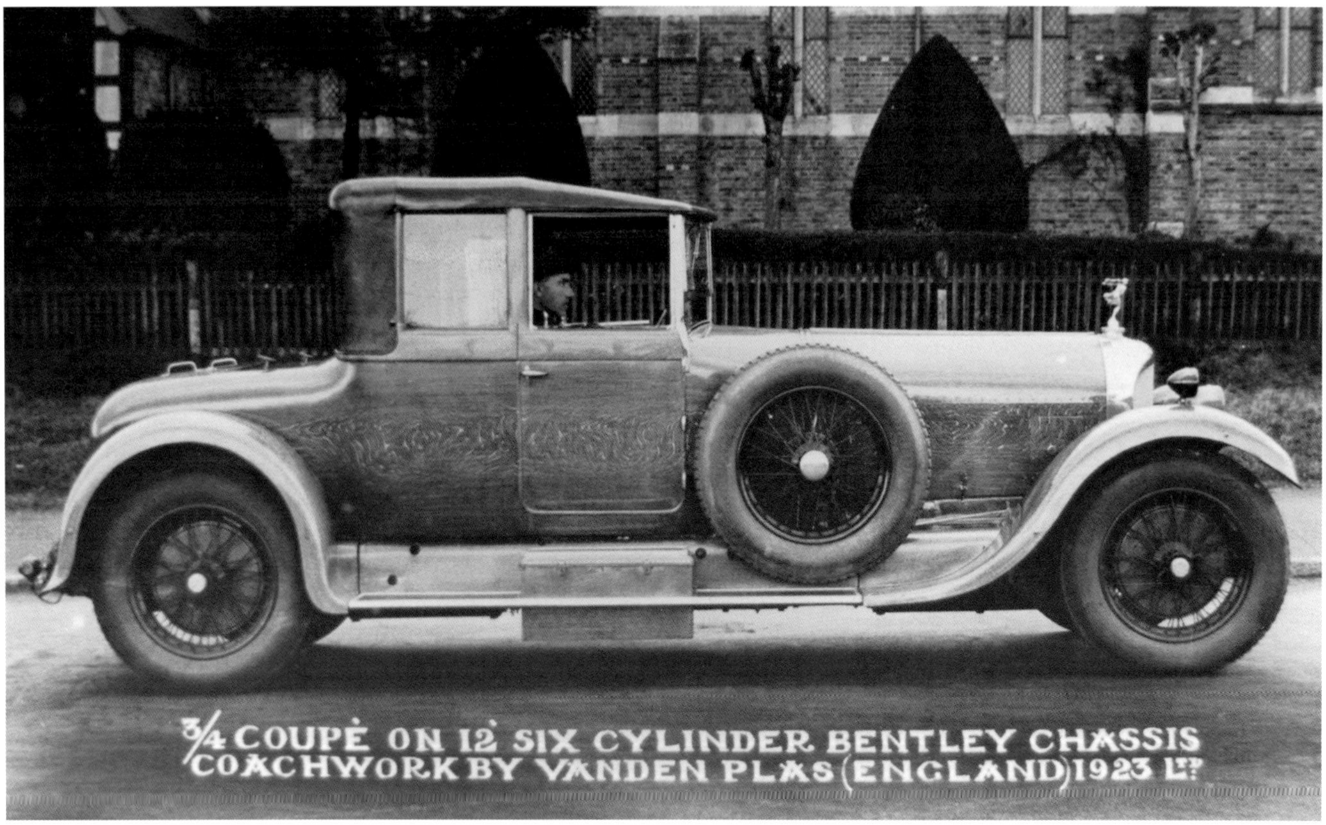

Another 6½ Litre chassis, TB2532, although unremarkable in other respects, shows an example of the craze for wood-graining, a much-admired finish at the time. The description "three-quarter coupé" implies there is a window behind the door, and means there was a complicated system for dropping the pillar between the two.

Another 1926 6½ Litre drophead coupé, this time from H J Mulliner. This design has all the hallmarks of one from the end of the decade. Its boot area is much better integrated into the rest of the form, and the back-sloping screen has built-in panes which we would nowadays call front quarter-lights.

For a 1926 car on the 6½ Litre chassis, this is something of a dinosaur. There can be no doubt about the balance and elegance of the overall design, but – although it is hard to spot – it is in fact a landaulet, where the rear portion of the hood folds down. The design is by Gurney Nutting, thought to be on chassis TB2529.

The coachbuilder of this smart 2/3-seater on a 1926 Speed Model Three Litre chassis is unknown, but it could well have been H J Mulliner. The designer has managed to make the lines attractive even with the hood erected.

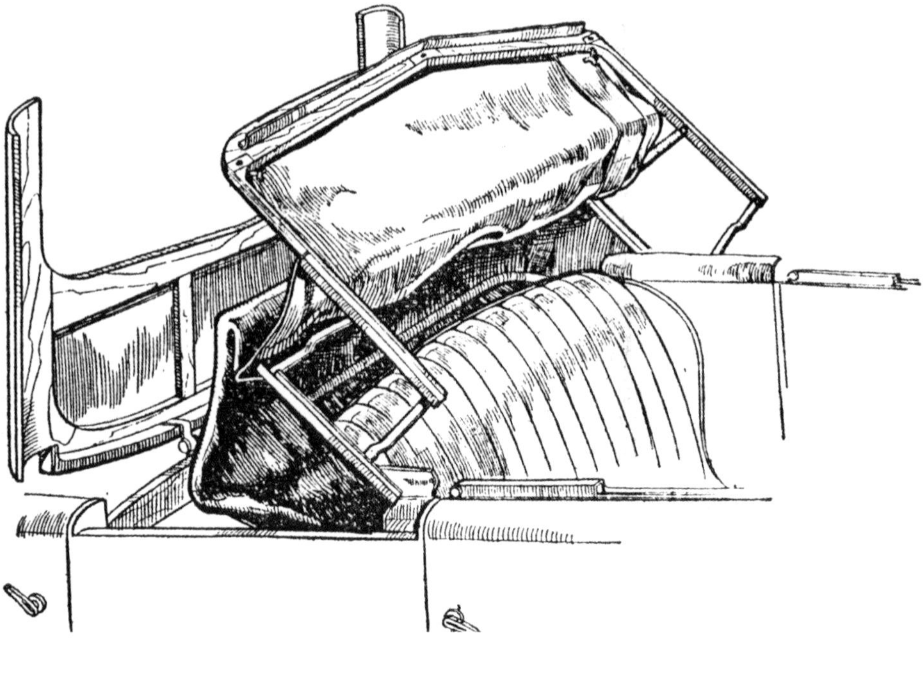

Offord were well-respected London coachbuilders but did little work on Bentleys. The drawing illustrates their neat disappearing hood on Three Litre chassis TN1566 of 1927.

This set of photos is of an early Three Litre from 1924, chassis 478, with a landaulet body by Park Ward. At first glance the car gives every appearance of being a limousine.

Even from the rear it is hard to detect the split in the roof where the rear portion can be detached.

Windscreen wipers were an advanced feature in 1924. Note also the useful parcel-net in the roof.

The Bentley motif is in evidence on the map pockets in all four doors.

Park Ward were only four years old when they built this body, but they had already established a high reputation.

In the closed position, the only clues to the car's body style are the ridge towards the rear of the roof and the unusual position of the carriage lamps. However as soon as the sun comes out the rear passengers can arrange things so that they are in the open air.

The dashboard plate, and the speedometer calibrated in both mph and kph, are explained by the first owner being resident in France. Carriage lamps were by this time an affectation rather than being of any practical value. Internal and external door handles are typical of the period.

The head folds flat to give good all-round visibility. Note the latches on the inside of the head, which lock the head to the fixed roof in the closed position.

There is a huge amount of legroom in the rear compartment. While the door windows have winding handles, the quarter-light glasses are operated by the older "strap and peg" system. Even with the occasional seats in use there is enough legroom for everyone.

This is a "D-division", curved to fit the back of the front seats, and with sliding glass panels for communication.

The driving position can only be described as "commanding". Note the two-panel windscreen, allowing the upper half to be opened for either ventilation or demisting.

Freestone & Webb were more often associated with saloons, but this drophead coupé (6½ Litre chassis TW2702 of late1926) shows that they were equally competent when it came to open cars. The Weymann construction is, unusually, covered not in fabric but in leather.

A body style favoured by the smart London set was variously known as "coupé de ville" or "sedanca de ville". This is thought to be the 1927 Olympia Show exhibit from Freestone & Webb, on 6½ Litre chassis BX2403. It was constructed on orthodox rather than Weymann principles. The lower picture shows how the "canopy" – that part of the roof over the driver's compartment – could be drawn back to give him an excess of air while his passengers stayed snug and warm. A typically impressive design from this talented company.

Here is another open design from Freestone & Webb, this time a drophead coupé on Three Litre Speed chassis TN1568 from early 1927. This is a modern restoration, but a faithful one, and the owner is to be praised for resisting the temptation to convert the car into another Le Mans replica.

The interior shot shows the high standard of restoration, and also reminds us of the forest of levers (handbrake and gear) which a driver's legs had to negotiate before he could sit down.

The chassis number of this 6½ Litre has not been identified, but the photograph dates it to the middle of 1927. In terms of body styles it makes an interesting comparison with the body shown at the top of page 94, illustrating the difference between a single coupé (as here) and a three-quarter coupé with a window behind the door.

William Arnold of Manchester were another very fine provincial coachbuilding firm. This drophead coupé on 6½ Litre chassis PR2320 is an excellent example of their work, giving a much better appearance with the hood up than many of their contemporaries.

Vanden Plas were better known for tourers than for drophead coupés, but this example, 4½ Litre chassis RN3041 from early 1928, shows some original thinking on their part. Recognising that most of the time only two seats will be used, they provided two sideways-facing seats for use in emergencies. The great advantage was of course that these extra seats were protected by the hood when it was raised.

From late 1928 we have Park Ward's version of a coupé de ville, thought to be on chassis FA2524. The wheel trims and bonnet are in polished aluminium, no doubt on the principle that if you're going to make a statement with a car like this you may as well do it properly.

By 1928 the heavily-peaked roof was becoming fashionable, and this Rippon drophead coupé on a 4½ Litre chassis shows the feature very well. Roof lines were also getting lower, which made it more difficult for the hood to reach across the front compartment…

…hence the complicated mechanism seen here. The running-boards are higher than was formally the fashion, partly to conceal the chassis and partly to avoid an excessively deep door. Ironically, later in the 1930s Rippon became known for their very low running-boards.

In late 1928 Motor Bodies of Newcastle produced this "three-quarter" drophead coupé on 6½ Litre chassis WT2271. Although the hood design is somewhat old-fashioned for the time there are advanced features as well, such as the peaked roof and the high boot-line.

Although this Freestone & Webb Weymann body, on the long 6½ Litre chassis (LB2345), was registered as a saloon, it is actually a landaulet as can be seen from the catches at the rear of the roof. Outdated though it may have been at the time – early 1929 – it is still a mightily impressive car, right down to the initials of its first owner Mr V E Gluckstein on the rear door.

Quite apart from their "Tickford" winding-handle head, the Salmons company made a speciality of drophead cars. This coupé is on $4^1/_2$ Litre chassis AB3373, from mid-1929, and once again it sports the newly-fashionable outside stretchers.

From the same period, in the middle 1929, comes this drophead coupé built by Martin Walter of Folkestone on $4^1/_2$ Litre chassis HB3405. The square hood and dickey-seat are more traditional, yet the general lines of the car and the high boot-line are bang up-to-date. Note the swage line running through the centre of the wings.

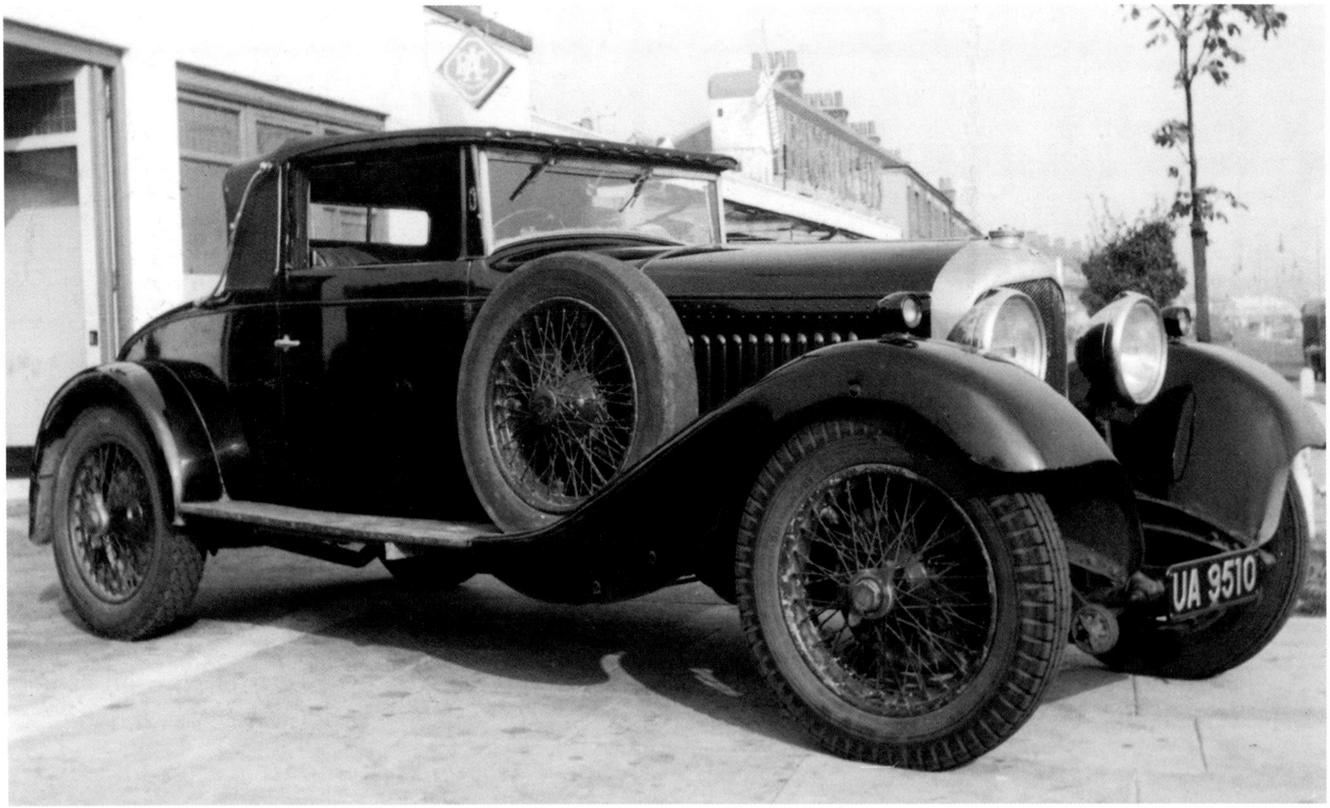

Carlton Carriage were yet another coachbuilder who increasingly specialised in drophead coupés. There is little remarkable about this 1929 design, on 4½ Litre chassis DS3562, except for the exaggerated valances on the front wings.

What a contrast after the last three drophead coupés! Freestone & Webb, always the innovators, threw away the concept of a combined dickey-seat and boot and in one move heralded the start of the 1930s. This design on Speed Six chassis FR2650, dating from mid 1929, set the tone for many other drophead coupé designs in the ensuing period, and heralded the gradual convergence of drophead and tourer styles.

The H J Mulliner sedanca de ville shown here was on their stand at the 1929 Olympia Show. It is on 6½ Litre chassis KR2687, and it bears all the hallmarks of that innate sense of balance which H J Mulliner designs possessed.

Very much a rarity, this Speed Six chassis SB2769 was bodied by the French coachbuilder Saoutchik. The body has been preserved and restored in its original state. Note the vee-windscreen, which most British coachbuilders had dropped by this date (end 1929).

Lancefield produced some outstanding designs, but it has to be said that this drophead coupé was not one of them. Apart from the outside hood-stretchers, it could have come from any time in the five years previous to early1930, when it is believed to have been built. It is thought to be 4½ Litre chassis PB3545.

Gurney Nutting's "sedanca coupé de ville" on Eight Litre chassis YF5004 bears so much polished aluminium and chrome that it borders on the vulgar, but as it was their 1930 Olympia Show car perhaps they can be excused. Otherwise the design is impeccable, and bang up-to-date with its domed wings, steps instead of running-boards and windscreen, door, bonnet-line and louvres all sloping in parallel. The construction could well be "semi-Weymann", since the roof appears to be covered in the shiny tole souple fabric.

Although the photo is modern, this car's restoration has been faithful to its original coachwork. Its domed wings show the influence of the "helmet" style then popular on tourer bodies. The luggage accommodation is tiny This is a 1930 Speed Six, chassis LR 2776, fitted with H J Mulliner drophead coupé coachwork.

Welcome to the streamlined era! The famous Barker "cabriolet" of mid-1931 (Eight Litre chassis YR5099) possesses all the talking-points of streamlining at that time – parabolic wings, float-type running-boards and a boat tail. Together these probably made little or no difference to the car's air-resistance, but they certainly turned it into an iconic design statement.

This is a Vanden Plas drophead coupé on Four Litre chassis VA4079, produced in early 1932 which was well after the sale of the old Bentley firm. Although not very pretty with its hood up, it carries the then-current fashion items for an open car, namely helmet wings and steps rather than running-boards. Note, too, how the rear deck has become raised to line up with the bonnet.

Although apparently out of chronological sequence, this 1928 4½ Litre chassis AB3351 was rebodied by Salmons in 1932 as a so-called all-weather, meaning that it bears their Tickford head, raised and lowered with a winding-handle. The photographs show the head in open and closed positions, and one can see the apparent watertight nature of the car when closed.

Chapter Three

Tourers and All-weathers

Even more than the cabriolet or drophead coupé, the touring body or "tourer" is the style which trend-setting owners and designers chose over the years to make their fashion statements. The truth of this has been evident from the early days of motoring right up to the last flowering of dramatic coachbuilt bodies in the 10 years after World War Two. In this chapter we shall examine the origin of the tourer body in the first decade of the last century, its relationship with sports and even racing styles, and how it came to replace the early "all-weather" styles which had no sporting pretensions at all.

In the very early years of car bodywork design there was little emphasis on overall appearance; it seemed to be accepted that the body was some sort of functional afterthought and that its shape was dictated by necessity. Nevertheless by, say, 1906 there had emerged a definite resistance to some of the more extreme features of car bodies as they then existed – low dashboards, high backs and so on. A low dashboard had been a logical consequence of the chassis being supplied with a low bonnet, and the designers' immediate reaction to the criticism – raising the height of the dashboard – led to cars with an even more bizarre appearance.

Eventually the coachbuilders seem to have prevailed on the chassis manufacturers to help them out, and chassis began to be delivered with the bonnet line raised significantly. Once this feature was established, and given the tendency to raise door heights and to lower the line of the back, the logical outcome was what became known as the "torpedo" body. Its invention has been traditionally been ascribed to Capt Masui (later the instigator of Van den Plas body production in Britain), who in late 1908 commissioned such a design on a Grégoire chassis. His claim to have originated the style, and in particular his attempt to patent it, was disputed by Cann, the coachbuilders in question, who believed that it all began from a sketch which they had supplied to the Captain.

Whatever the rights and wrongs, there can be no doubt about the influence which the torpedo had on the development of car design. Within a very short time car bodywork had transformed itself from tall, ungainly shapes to sleek, low ones – low, that is, within the context of the times. A torpedo was always an open body, what we would now call a tourer. Its key feature was that the bonnet, the waistline and the top of the rear panel formed a continuous horizontal line. A secondary characteristic was that the side panels were slightly convex, something which Barker exploited and exaggerated some years later in their "barrel-bodied" tourers. Neither feature was so easy to achieve in limousines or landaulets, since their more upright seats demanded higher doors.

At about the same time as the torpedo style was invented, the term "all-weather" seems to have come into use and was immediately seized on by the coachbuilding industry. Such a description clearly evoked everything the motorist of the time felt that he was looking for – a good-size body which could be as snug as a limousine in inclement weather and yet which would allow him the freedom of the open air at a moment's notice. By 1910 an all-weather body clearly meant one with a "Cape cart" hood (ie covering the front seats as well as the back), folding vertical pillars and window-glass dropping into the body framework. Importantly, it was also differentiated from the tourer by having a much higher standard of internal trim and fittings. It differed from the cabriolet of the time firstly by having no glass division and secondly by enclosing the driver's seat, leading the firm of William Cole to describe their model perversely as an "interior driving sociable cabriolet"!

Considerable work now went into the development of all-weather bodies, and into the specialist fittings which would make them progressively easier to handle. The "Kopalapso" hood, for example, was an ingenious design of framework which allowed the hood to fold on to itself and take up the minimum amount of room. It was an early answer to the perpetual desire for the so-called "one-man hood". A similar solution was the use of folding cant-rails, which again prevented the folded hood overhanging the body and which remained a feature of all-weathers, cabriolets and drophead coupés right up to recent times.

Yet there were doubters who wondered whether a single body style would ever totally satisfy the conflicting demands for open air in good weather and comfort in bad. A writer in 1913 made a prophetic, if long-winded, observation on the relative attractions of open cars and what he called "saloon limousines" (in other words saloons): "It is open to argument whether there is really much demand for a double purpose body, as the saloon limousine is rapidly gaining in popularity, and if, as seems likely, a body of this type can be turned out at a competitive price it is pretty well bound to supersede a body of the convertible type, especially as people are beginning to realise that with an all-enclosed limousine with the windows down one can have practically an open car with none of the rattlesomeness and certainly more comfort than any convertible body can possibly give one."

The motoring commentator Owen John, writing in 1919, made a similar point, although somewhat more cynically: "I am struck by the number of owners who complain to me that they are not in love with their car bodies when they try to be all things to all men, as it were, and pose as perfection whether they be open or shut. Finality, in their opinion, has not yet been attained: indeed, the only man who is pleased with his *en tout cas* is one who is so satisfied with it as a shut car that he cannot now open it if he tried. He says all the sides open and shut as windows, and that the top is equally useful to keep the rain or the sun from his head. He drives himself always, and therefore is in no need to bother about having his man inside with him. Why, he asks, should he want to keep opening and shutting the thing? It will only begin to rattle when he does. So he keeps it permanently closed."

Once the tourer body had established itself as the leader of design with its new torpedo shape, it looked around for somewhere new to go. It seems to have occurred to more than one designer that the new shape resembled a boat as much as a torpedo, and "boat-shaped" was indeed used as an alternative description. This was not enough, however, and it became increasingly tempting to design a tourer to look as much like a boat as possible. One of the most extreme attempts, it must be said, was also one of the very earliest. In 1909 the Earl of Shrewbury and Talbot commissioned Rothschild to build a body which, being pointed at both ends, looked like nothing so much as a lifeboat mounted on a car chassis. Later, when a degree of sanity had returned, clients contented themselves with designs which were pointed at the rear only. However, they compensated by making the nautical resemblance as close as possible.

It has to be admitted that, in this instance as in so many other fashions in coachwork, it was the French who took things to the limit. Indeed it is possible that the whole idea started as some kind of Parisian joke. The very first design, built by Labourdette in 1912, was commissioned by Chevalier René de Knyff, managing director of Panhard et Levassor and a well-known racing driver. When Labourdette asked him why his proposed design had no doors, de Knyff's reply was that by making the ladies climb over the side he would be able to see their legs!

At the Paris Salon in 1913 there were countless variations on the "skiff torpedo" theme – almost all with pointed tails, and all with as many nautical references as possible. Natural wood finishes, wooden ribbed interiors and dummy copper rivets were taken as normal. To be noticed one had to add such features as side-lamps shaped like ship's ventilators, or door-handles like rowlocks. One exhibit had cushions shaped like fenders, with ropes attached. British coachbuilders affected to be unimpressed, and although some produced their own skiff designs the fashion did not properly cross the Channel until the early 1920s.

Thus by the time the first Bentleys were coming

on to the market, the tourer was well-established as a popular design. In its more luxurious form it was still often called an "all-weather", while the more spartan versions – particularly if they were two-seaters – would be given the "sporting" tag. At the lower end of the market there was more confusion. Tourers up to then had been given very little weather protection, but the advent of rigid, remove-able side-curtains (pioneered by the Standard company) improved the public's perceptions of such cars. They continued to use the popular Kopalapso head, or the later Gwynne head where the previous heavy wood hood sticks were replaced with slimmer, lighter steel ones. Unfortunately the manufacturers chose to call this new style an "all-weather", and it was some years before the "tourer" description became more common.

The Gwynne head came to the market in 1921, and caused quite a stir at that year's Olympia Show. *The Autocar* said that it "embodies a principle unique in collapsible tops ...The whole of the framework of this top is made up with a special light metal channelling in combination with drawn steel tubes, used as a substitute for heavy woodwork, so that for a 12hp car the total weight of the whole fitting, without glass, is but 42lbs [19kg]. Neverthe-less, with this lightness, absolute rigidity, great strength, and freedom of working of all moving parts are obtained, while in driving over the roughest roads at high speed, we are able to testify, there is no rattle or noise, while the hood can be raised or lowered when driving at ordinary touring speed."

One can see this transition between the early all-weather style and the later tourer in an exhibit on the Vanden Plas stand at the 1922 Olympia Show. A report at the time drew attention to "an excellent feature in the all-weather body", namely "the means by which the centre head stick is secured to the centre pillars by wing nuts". By implication the hood was the comparatively flimsy type which we associate with tourers, but the style retained the old-fashioned folding pillars. The reporter's judgement was that the device "overcomes a common defect in this class of hood".

Soon it became apparent that buyers of tourers, particularly on upmarket chassis such as the Bentley, were more and more the diehard type. Their priority was a light body which would not noticeably impair the car's performance, and passenger comfort took second place. Those who wanted their car to be totally dry and comfortable in wet weather could order a cabriolet or a drophead coupé. It would appear that the diehards' passengers did not always share their enthusiasm, judging from the plaintive cries in the motoring press for better weather protection in the back of such cars.

The Autocar was particularly vocal on behalf of the oppressed rear-seat passengers. In a 1921 article titled "Protecting the Rear Passengers" they set out the argument in some detail. "For some time we have focussed attention upon the necessity for some special protection for the occupants of the rear seats of open touring cars…The problem is not altogether an easy one, for it is not merely sufficient to add a second windscreen behind the front seats, for, unless the position of this second screen is chosen with some care, the disadvantages may out weigh the advantages offered. In general, the rear screen should be as close to the occupants of the rear seat as possible; otherwise, not only will the protection afforded them prove inadequate, but the back draught from the front screen, which proves so unpleasant on some cars to the occupants of the front seat, will be considerably emphasised, with the nett result that the rear passengers are but partly protected, while the front passengers are much inconvenienced. There is also the question of ease of ingress and egress, for the door of the rear compart-ment must necessarily be far enough forward to clear the rear wing."

Strangely, passengers were worse off in the back of a coachbuilt tourer than in a cheaper car, if only because in the more expensive (and therefore bigger) models they were further away from the windscreen. Eventually such devices as the Beatonson or Auster screen, which could be folded out from behind the front seats, came to their rescue. Some of these would also convert into a division, thus preserving the social niceties between chauffeur and employer when the car was in its closed form.

An alternative version of the rear screen was attached to a separate hinged flap, which could be folded up out of the way to permit the rear passen-gers to alight more gracefully. In effect this produced the style known in America as the "twin-cowl phaeton". H J Mulliner exhibited one such design at the 1923 London Show, and it caught the eye of a *Motor* reporter: "A very attractive touring body is shown on a Bentley chassis. A noteworthy feature of this is a balanced hinging back scuttle, which affords the rear passengers full protection from the elements. There are two windscreens, both fitted with side wings, while the sides of the body are high and the seating low".

Other so-called "sporting" models this same year

were to be seen on the stands of Page & Hunt – "a good example of sports coachwork ... the body being painted silver-grey with green wings and upholstered in green leather" – and Park Ward: "A two-door all-weather body ... painted smoke blue, the wings being finished black and the upholstery being effected in brown leather covering self-controlled air cushions. The front seats fold, slide, and tip. Patent window lifts are fitted, and a feature worth special notice is the light-section metal pillars of the V-front which allow practically unrestricted all-round view".

The emphasis is, quite clearly, still at this stage much more on comfort than lightness and performance, although Park Ward were quite capable of producing the latter if required. The firm's two founders, William MacDonald Park and Charles W Ward, had acquired considerable experience in the industry, latterly at the Sizaire-Berwick London factory, before they set up in business in 1919 at Willesden, north-west London. Clearly both ambitious and successful, the partners were already exhibiting at Olympia the following year, and by 1923 were bodying the first of many Bentleys – 143 in all. They had already been permitted to body Rolls-Royce chassis, from as early as 1920, and these two marques came to dominate Park Ward's output for the rest of the decade. When the Bentley work disappeared temporarily in 1931, their connection with Rolls-Royce stood them in good stead, with that company eventually buying first a minority shareholding and then the entire company.

By 1924 the balance between comfort and performance was coming down in favour of lighter methods of construction. At the Olympia Show that year Charlesworth exhibited a "sports model four-seater body with two front doors" which, importantly, had no "side curtains" – just a Cape hood (that is, one which reached over both rows of seats and fixed to the windscreen). Gurney Nutting were reluctant to go this far, but a year later provided lightweight side-screens which could be removed and stored in a recess behind the driver's seat.

This was the point when cellulose paints began to be used. In 1926 it was reported that the year's predominant colours were black, grey, green, brown, red, dark blue, primrose, and ivory. We can clearly see the influence of cellulose in the last two, although some still preferred the effect of no paint at all – what was described as "scratched aluminium varnished". At the same time boat bodies made yet another comeback, typified by Barker's exhibit at that year's Show: "Another striking model is the boat-shaped three-seater body on a Bentley, with a hood which, when not in use, is concealed on both sides of the cockpit. This body is exquisitely finished in cream with the top deck in walnut, the upholstery being in brown leather."

From the same coachbuilder (Barker) two years later there was another striking colour scheme: "A sports two-four-seater on a Bentley 6½ Litre is also cellulose-finished in Olympia yellow, but the top of the bonnet and scuttle and the bonnet louvres are in burnished aluminium, while the wings, wheels and chassis are in blue to match the leather upholstery. Streamline wings and tool boxes and a concealed hood are interesting points." The reference to streamlining is highly significant, since the streamline movement – possibly the single most important influence on the aesthetic design of cars between the wars – grew dramatically during the 1920s, even though it was not to come to full fruition until the following decade.

Although there were a number of early intuitive attempts at producing a streamlined body, it was only after World War 1 that scientific experiment took over. It was in 1921 that Paul Jaray began testing scale models of car bodies, using the wind-tunnel at the Zeppelin airship works where he was chief engineer. In the following two years the Zeppelin company made at least three prototypes, using Ley chassis, presumably to test public reaction. Since the cars did not go into production, one can only assume that they were found to be too radical to be acceptable; this was in spite of the fact that their engines were in the conventional position at the front, which made them far less outlandish in appearance than some of the rear-engined experiments which were to follow. Jaray's cars nevertheless had the distinction of a true teardrop tail - ie one which tapered in both plan and elevation.

At the same time (1921), another aircraft engineer was testing prototypes in another wind-tunnel. Dr Edmund Rumpler used the Eiffel laboratory at Auteuil in France, to test his prototypes. From a technical point of view these were highly advanced: the engines were placed at the rear, to keep the car's width to a minimum at this point, and their six cylinders were arranged in a novel "broad-arrow" configuration to minimise overall length. Moreover, Rumpler developed his own swing-axle suspension at the rear. The arrangement gave an approximation to a teardrop shape in plan, but not in elevation (although the open sports version was much closer to this ideal than the saloon, and prettier as well). Further reductions in drag were achieved by concealing the springs (four semi-elliptics) within the bodywork, and by using solid-disc wheels and minimal mudguards.

Rumpler's work did at least produce some results, since the startling rear-engined Benz Grand Prix cars, entered at Monza in 1923, were based on his work. In fact, however, Benz only used the swing-axle portion of his design; the engines were in-line sixes, with the transmission being behind and in unit with the crankcase. They also brought the radiator outside the main body shell, sacrificing aerodynamics for cooling capacity. This seems to have been the end of the road for Rumpler's design, and no more was heard of it.

Whatever the fate of their particular prototypes, these two men, Jaray and Rumpler, seem to have determined later designers' thinking about streamlining. Both assumed unswervingly that the teardrop shape was essential, even though later scientific study shown it to be a false assumption. Rumpler went further and assumed that this shape could only be achieved with a rear-engined configuration. From the early 1920s on, therefore, this rear-engine fixation ruled any discussion about streamlining. Next to fall in line was Sir Dennistoun Burney, at the time (1928) Chief Designer of the Vickers R101 airship at Howden in Yorkshire. Presumably in his spare time, he designed and built a prototype streamlined car, based on a (reversed) Alvis front-wheel drive chassis; later cars were powered by Beverley-Barnes, Lycoming and Armstrong-Siddeley engines. The design certainly approximated to the desired teardrop shape, but showed the other typical characteristics of these rear-engined exercises: poor rearward visibility and unattractive - some would say ugly - lines. In fairness to Burney, his devotion to the teardrop was based not only on aerodynamic reasons, but also on his theories of optimum mass-distribution for passenger comfort.

Given the emphasis from these experts on the necessity for rear-engined chassis for streamlining, it is not surprising that the British coachbuilding industry steered clear of fully streamlined designs during the 1920s. None of their clients, however anxious to make an impression at the next concours d'élégance, was sufficiently brave to order a streamlined body, even on a conventional front-engined chassis. Nevertheless, the industry and its clients did take note of the streamlining movement, and would often describe a design in such terms even though it bore no relation to a teardrop shape. Moreover, there was an increasing tendency to give the teardrop treatment to individual parts of the body, starting with the tail - hence the many "boat-tail" designs, as we have already seen. Other areas subjected to streamlining at this time were such things as "float-type" running-boards, "flared" wings (the vestigial, eyebrow-type wings popular on mid-1920s sports cars) and, later, "swept" wings which continued in an unbroken line to form the running-board. Windscreens were sloped back, peaked roofs were made peakless ("eddy-free"), and sunshine roofs were made flush-fitting, all in the name of streamlining.

Designers were faced at around the same time, the late 1920s, with another in-vogue feature: lengthened bonnets. One has to accept that this was entirely a fashion-driven move, since there are no obvious technical reasons for it to have happened. No doubt it was motivated in part by the streamlining craze. More importantly, however, a longer bonnet suggested racing-car design and therefore power. Designers resorted to new levels of inventiveness to make their bonnets appear longer. The easiest way was to extend the bonnet over the scuttle, and the next was to move the scuttle itself – with the windscreen – further back, while leaving the seats where they were (which did nothing for ease of access). The front seats themselves, incidentally, were by now generally adjustable fore-and-aft, the well-known "Leveroll" mechanism having been introduced two years earlier; adjustable back seats were by no means uncommon either. Pneumatic cushions were being increasingly used in smaller or lower bodies where the room for stuffed spring-cases, or even foam rubber, was limited.

Even now the "tourer versus all-weather" argument had not died. Writing in *The Motor* in 1926, coachwork expert H J Butler set out the arguments for and against both. "The ordinary four-door four-light all-weather body gives better protection from the weather when the hood is up than a touring body, because the windows rise and fall in grooves or runs and do not merely overlap. Also the use of glass instead of celluloid gives a clearer outlook, especially when a comparison is made after extended use. Another advantage of the all-weather body is that it can be ventilated by lowering the windows, and, by a skilful adjustment on the leeward side, maintain a supply of fresh air even in bad weather. Many motorists, however, do not consider the absence of good ventilation of the fully protected car or the want of transparency of worn side screens a disadvantage serious enough to warrant paying the extra price asked for the average four-door all-weather. The motorist will readily admit that it is a trouble to detach the side screens and pack them away, and often he proves the truth of his assertion, because he is quite content to leave them in position, especially as he finds that the comfort of driving is increased thereby."

Tourer coachwork at the end of the decade was typified by a 6½-litre Bentley two-seater bodied by Park Ward and reviewed (and pictured) in *The Autocar* in August 1929. "Streamlined wings are a feature", it said. "To tone with these wings the running boards are also streamlined and have the appearance of aeroplane floats. In them are carried the tools. Features of this body are the extended bonnet, which runs right up to the windscreen, a concealed hood, a two-seater dickey, and accommodation for spare wheels in the rear of the body." In a similar vein was this description of a Vanden Plas exhibit at the Olympia Show that same year: "Very attractive is the sporting four-seater Speed Model Bentley finished in myrtle green fabric with a pigskin covered moulding running along bonnet and body. The upholstery is in pigskin and affords the maximum amount of comfort. The screen is of three-panel type with triplex glass and the hood is covered in mohair to match the upholstery. Cycle-type wings give the car a sporting appearance." Clearly even the tourer diehards – or at least those amongst them who could afford a Bentley – liked a certain amount of comfort.

The reference to cycle wings recalls that curious, and quite short-lived, period towards the end of the 1920s, to which we have referred earlier. This was the adoption of "cycle" or "helmet" style front wings, and the consequent removal of running-boards and their replacement by a simple metal step. This, it will be remembered, required the invention of a new device, the chassis valance. Where bodywork of a sporting nature was involved, designers frequently decorated the chassis valance with louvres, not for any functional purpose but merely for aesthetic reasons. Possibly louvres also suggested that the car sported an undertray, which in turn smacked of a racing pedigree.

We have previously referred to another significant development at this period – the desire to reduce a car's overall height. This was achieved either by providing foot-wells for the rear passengers, or by lowering the chassis, or both. Underslung, downswept or "dropped" chassis became the norm by the end of the twenties, and Bentley were no exception with the introduction of the Eight Litre model. One immediate effect could be seen in the design of sports bodies: their drivers could no longer reach over the door either to operate an outside handbrake or to give a hand-signal, and this change more than anything brought about the birth of the cutaway sportscar door.

What, one may ask, is a mid-1930s body doing here? Surprisingly, this is the first body put on this chassis (RC44), one of a short run of 4½ Litre cars which were built up from the remaining stock of new parts. Vanden Plas built it in 1936.

This is a very early Three Litre tourer, chassis 84, and its body is by one of the rarer coachbuilders, Lawton (also known as Lawton-Goodman). As can be seen from the glossy finish, it predates by a long way the Weymann era. The helmet-style wings are interesting, as they went out of fashion almost immediately and then came back later in the decade.

The Gwynne head, which was invented by the James Young coachbuilding company, was sold to car manufacturers Gwynne who then sold it on to accessory manufacturer Beatonson. By using metal rather than wooden hood-sticks it reduced the weight of the hood structure considerably, and so prolonged the life of the all-weather style.

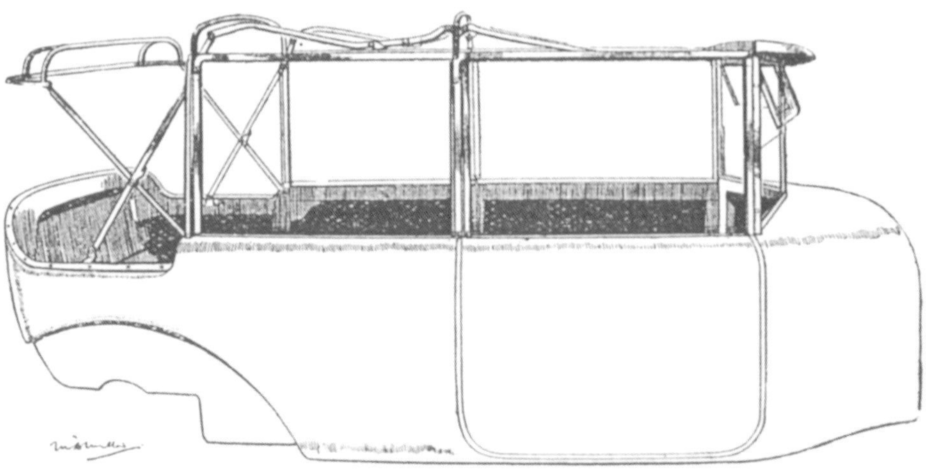

It has not been possible to identify this Three Litre chassis, but it probably dates from the 1922 era. Although at first glance the body, built by Harrison of Dewsbury in Yorkshire, could be mistaken for a saloon, it is in fact an "all-weather" as can be seen from the picture below. This style has a hood which covers both front and rear compartments and a complicated system of pillars for the side windows. These either fold down or (as in this case) retract with the hood once the windows are wound down inside the doors.

This is Three Litre chassis 142 from 1922, coachbuilder unknown, and it is a good example of the clover-leaf style which had two seats in front and one at the rear. This allowed the tail to be given a pointed shape, often known as a boat tail.

This Three Litre tourer is another rare bird, having been bodied by the Birmingham coachbuilder Buckingham. It is chassis 277 from mid-1923, and uses the vestigial swept front wings so beloved of the sporting fraternity at that time.

Here is Three Litre Speed Model chassis 415 being used in earnest up a hill in Honiton, Devon. The coachbuilder is not known, but he succeded in producing a stylish body with very attractive flared wings front and back.

Vanden Plas are of course best known for their four-seater tourers, but this picture gives evidence that they were just as much at home with the two-seater sports style. This is Three Litre Speed Model chassis 431 from late 1923.

More representative of a typical Vanden Plas tourer is this early Three Litre four-seater. The chassis is not known, but it probably dates from around 1924. The absence of a driver's door is a common feature of Vanden Plas tourers.

William Arnold of Manchester were another provincial coachbuilder whose products bore comparison with the best London firms, in both design and execution. For the beginning of 1924 this all-weather, on Three Litre chassis 444, is remarkably stylish.

We have to thank Park Ward for this attractive tourer from early 1924. It is on Three Litre chassis 544, and has been restored to its original condition. Note the complex rear screen arrangement for back-seat passengers, essential with such a long car.

This unknown Three Litre chassis was bodied by Freestone & Webb in early 1925. It shows significant differences from the previous Park Ward example, particularly in its "barrel-sided" curvature and in the much more substantial pillar between the two doors.

By 1925 the Bentley company were trying to standardise different styles of coachwork. This "Three Litre Short Standard Tourer" was produced by Vanden Plas, and at the time was the cheapest Bentley available. Its short chassis (9' 9½") did nothing for its appearance.

Vanden Plas are credited with this very exciting-looking two-seater sports on Three Litre TT Replica chassis 263 dating from mid-1923. It is another example of the boat style of tail, a fashion which had developed before World War 1.

Here we find yet another boat-tailed sports Three Litre Speed Model (chassis 1050), but this time the coachbuilder was Jarvis of Wimbledon (even though the records ascribe it to Vanden Plas). It again dates from mid 1925.

This nicely-restored Three Litre Speed Model (chassis AH1482) was built by the Guildford firm of May & Jacobs, and dates from early 1926. The flimsy hood and light, removable side-screens are typical of tourers of the period.

Jarvis of Wimbledon, under the management of Arthur Compton, specialised in racy-looking sporting coachwork. They must have been delighted to get their hands on one of the early 6½ Litre chassis (WB2553) at the beginning of 1926. Note how the designer (probably Compton himself) has minimised the width of the body by offsetting the passenger's seat behind the driver's.

This is one of the famous "100 mph" Three Litre chassis, bodied in two-seater sports form by Vanden Plas and probably dating from early 1926. The tail has now gone beyond a typical boat shape and is tending to reflect the teardrop form beloved by streamlining theorists.

Although it has seen better days, the coachwork on this Three Litre Speed Model (chassis 1207) from early 1926 is interesting, being a very early example of a coming fashion for chassis valances. These became a kind of shorthand for sporting cars, suggesting maybe that the car had an undertray and therefore a sporting pedigree.

Thrupp & Maberly bodied this 6½ Litre chassis (WB 2563) in September 1926. The customer was an Indian nawab, and the car was to be used for big-game hunting – hence the lights on extending cable-reels and rifle cases on the running-boards.

For the 1926 Olympia Motor Show Barker built the first of several dramatic exhibits. This one is a Three Litre Speed Model, chassis LT1578, with a three-seat sports body. Although the body was later modified, it has since been returned to its original condition. The photograph shows the extraordinary walnut finish on the tail, and also a very early application of the streamlined running-board known as the "float" type.

This Vanden Plas three-seater sports design on Three Litre Speed Model chassis BL1604 is from early 1927. Apparently of Weymann construction, it shows the very advanced feature of the sloping windscreen matching a sloping door hinge-line. The effect would be for the door to rise as it is opened, but with Weymann bodies doors were so light that this made little difference.

This H J Mulliner body on the long 6½ Litre chassis KD2114 from mid-1927 is an "all-weather". This implies wind-up windows, which require standing pillars when they are closed; these can just be made out, attached to the hood-frame in such a way that they stand vertically when the hood is erected.

As opposed to the H J Mulliner car we have just seen, this Harrison body is a true tourer and, if it has any weather equipment at all, it will take the form of removable side-screens. Note the way in which the scuttle has been raised at the rear, to allow a higher waistline than normal (presumably for extra passenger protection). This is the mid-length 6½ Litre chassis MD2463, dating from early 1928.

Here an early 4½ Litre Vanden Plas tourer (HF3195, March 1928) is seen in its ideal setting, the Brooklands track, with a BARC member's sticker on the headlamp. Maybe our hero had been competing, which might account for the wear on the tyres.

A Harrison tourer on a $4^1/_2$ Litre chassis (HF3184). Although the panels appear to be fabric-covered, it is unlikely that the car is of Weymann construction as by this time, mid-1928, Harrison were wedded to their patent "British Flexible" system.

There is everything to be said for restoring these cars to the same standard, and the same specification, as when they left the factory. This is a Vanden Plas tourer on $4^1/_2$ Litre chassis TX3239, from mid-1928

This next set of pictures covers a 1926 Three Litre Speed Model, chassis 1236, with four-seater sports body by Jarvis of Wimbledon.

Above: Although the body has been restored, it still shows off its lines well. Only the wings have been replaced; although not identical, they are a close copy of the original ones.

Opposite: The tonneau cover is held in place by a pair of neat straps. In this configuration the car can be driven at reasonable speed in the rain with neither front nor rear compartments getting wet.

COACHWORK
DESIGNED
& BUILT BY
— JARVIS & SONS, LTD. —
WIMBLEDON
S.W.19.
'PHONE 2526.

The compound curves of the rear panelling have been particularly well handled. Note that there is a trace of "barrel-body" about the design, which makes a welcome contrast to other straight-sided tourers of the time.

The Wimbledon firm of Jarvis in the SW19 area of London were not to be confused with their lesser-known namesakes in Edgware Road, W2. This Jarvis had the renowned Arthur Compton as their designer during our period.

Here the tonneau cover is in place over the rear compartment. Note that there is only one door to serve the four occupants.

This is what the inside of the door looked like when new, and still does. The flap covers a map pocket.

Once seats were made lower, it was necessary to make a cut-out in the driver's "door" so that he could reach the outside handbrake. After handbrakes and gear-levers moved inside, the fashion continued.

The chassis number stamped on the inside of the bonnet shows that this was one item of bodywork made at the factory rather than by the coachbuilder.

Trim in sporting cars was relatively spartan, being little more than carpet laid on wooden boards.

This set covers a 1928 4½ Litre, chassis KM3087, with the classic Vanden Plas four-seater Weymann sports body. The design, although familiar to most of us, is nevertheless imposing.

The design also passes the test of looking good even with the hood up. This car is unchanged from when it was built, to the extent of retaining its original fabric covering.

This view probably gives the best impression as to how a Weymann body would have looked originally. The rear window, though, would have been significantly smaller.

The fabric covering used in the Weymann system extends over the scuttle but not the bonnet.

There is a roomy compartment for the rear-seat passengers – possibly too roomy, as the high seats and distance from the windscreen will make it a draughty place. Note that, unlike the Jarvis four-seater, this design boasts three doors.

A further authentic touch on this wonderfully original and unspoilt car is the Vanden Plas plaque attached to the door trim.

The hood is thin enough to pack flat in a separate bag – aided by the Vanden Plas hood frame. The tonneau cover fits over the bag.

Above: The fabric has obviously crazed over the years. There is provision for fitting side-screens, but most owners seem to prefer to leave the sides open.

Right: The outside handbrake makes another appearance, to emphasise the coachwork's sporting character.

Far right: The driver again has a cut-out in his "door". The decision not to add a driver's door assumes that he will prefer to slide out to the near side rather than clamber over the clutter of gear-lever and handbrake.

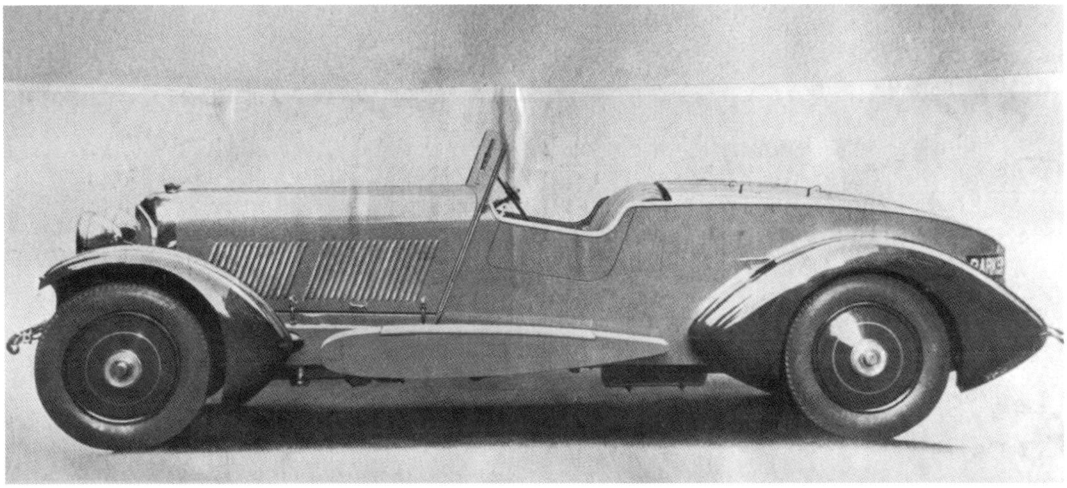

Another highly dramatic statement from Barker, designed to attract attention to their stand at the 1928 Olympia Show. It has all the characteristics demanded by the new craze for streamlining – parabolic wings, float-type running-boards and a teardrop tail. It even appears to have a dickey-seat.

The constructional details of the two-seater body by Vanden Plas fitted to "Birkin Blower" chassis HB3402 for the 1929 500-Miles race. The smaller ribs are metal, screwed to wooden framing.

Built for an Indian maharajah, this impressive H J Mulliner tourer from the beginning of 1929 is on long 6½ Litre chassis KF2389. Note the hinged flap on which the rear screen is mounted, which rear-seat passengers lift in order to gain access.

Although this Vanden Plas body is fabric-covered, it is not listed as a Weymann. It is on Speed Six chassis KF2399, from early 1929. Once again we see the hinged flap which covers the knees of rear-seat passengers and brings the rear screen closer to their faces. The tail treatment is unusual.

Another Harrison tourer makes an interesting comparison with the example we saw on page 136. This one is on Speed Six chassis BA2586 of mid-1929, and interestingly is for the same customer as a year earlier. Note how the previous scuttle curvature has been moved backwards to the leading edge of the front door.

Another streamlining extravaganza from Barker is sometimes said (wrongly) to have been at the 1929 London Show. We can now take for granted the parabolic wings, float-type running-boards and pointed tail. This is Speed Six chassis KF2400, from July 1929.

At about the same time, July 1929, Park Ward apparently decided to join the trend towards streamlining. The Barker influences are clear, and the only original features are the bonnet extended to the windscreen and the all-black finish. Two spare wheels are contained in the tail. This is Speed Six chassis FR2637.

A tourer from Vanden Plas, on 6½ Litre long chassis WT2264. It is finished in fabric, but likely to be of British Flexible construction rather than Weymann. This body dates from August 1929, and apart from the addition of a luggage trunk it has to be admitted that tourer design had hardly moved forward during the previous five years.

This is another example which has survived into the present day and been restored to its original condition. It is a Vanden Plas tourer on 4½ Litre chassis KL3578, originally a demonstrator which was then sold to Sir Malcolm Campbell. Some interest has been added to the design by giving the side panels some "turn-under" towards the bottom.

At last we find a significant change in tourer design. This is the Vanden Plas two-door that was on the Bentley stand at the 1930 London Motor Show. Essentially what has happened is that drophead coupé influences – largely from Freestone & Webb – have overwhelmed the previous tradition of four-seat tourer design. The car is 4½ Litre Supercharged chassis SM3920 from late 1930.

Another year, another Vanden Plas four-seat tourer. Luggage accommodation now seems here to stay, and the only other minor design change is that the running-boards have been raised somewhat. This was a common move among coachbuilders of the time, to try and minimise the apparent height of the car. The chassis is 4½ Litre KL3584, from January 1930.

It is interesting that when Woolf Barnato, the Bentley company's effective owner, wanted a 2/3-seater, he went not to Vanden Plas or Jarvis but to Gurney Nutting. This is one of the 4½ Litre Supercharged cars, chassis SM3909, and dates from July 1930.

Hooper were, by general consent, the best of the best, yet their products feature comparatively rarely on vintage Bentley chassis. This is one such example – Speed Six chassis LR2793, dating from July 1930

On the other hand there were some customers who liked their Bentley tourers just the way they always were. This is a traditional Vanden Plas design on 4½ Litre Supercharged chassis SM3923 from December 1930.

The arrival of the Eight Litre chassis gave coachbuilders even more scope than before (although not for very long). This version was described as a "four-seater", probably meaning that designers found it as difficult then as we do now to distinguish between tourers and drophead coupés. This chassis is YR5095 from June 1931, and was Woolf Barnato's personal propert

The Four Litre chassis, the last one produced by the old Bentley company, was of course identical to the Eight Litre in all important respects. The result, as on the Vanden Plas tourer here (thought to be chassis VF4021), was imposing if nothing else. This car was completed in November 1931, after the company had gone into receivership.

In complete contrast, this four-seater tourer was also offered by Vanden Plas on the Four Litre chassis; three examples are known to have been built.

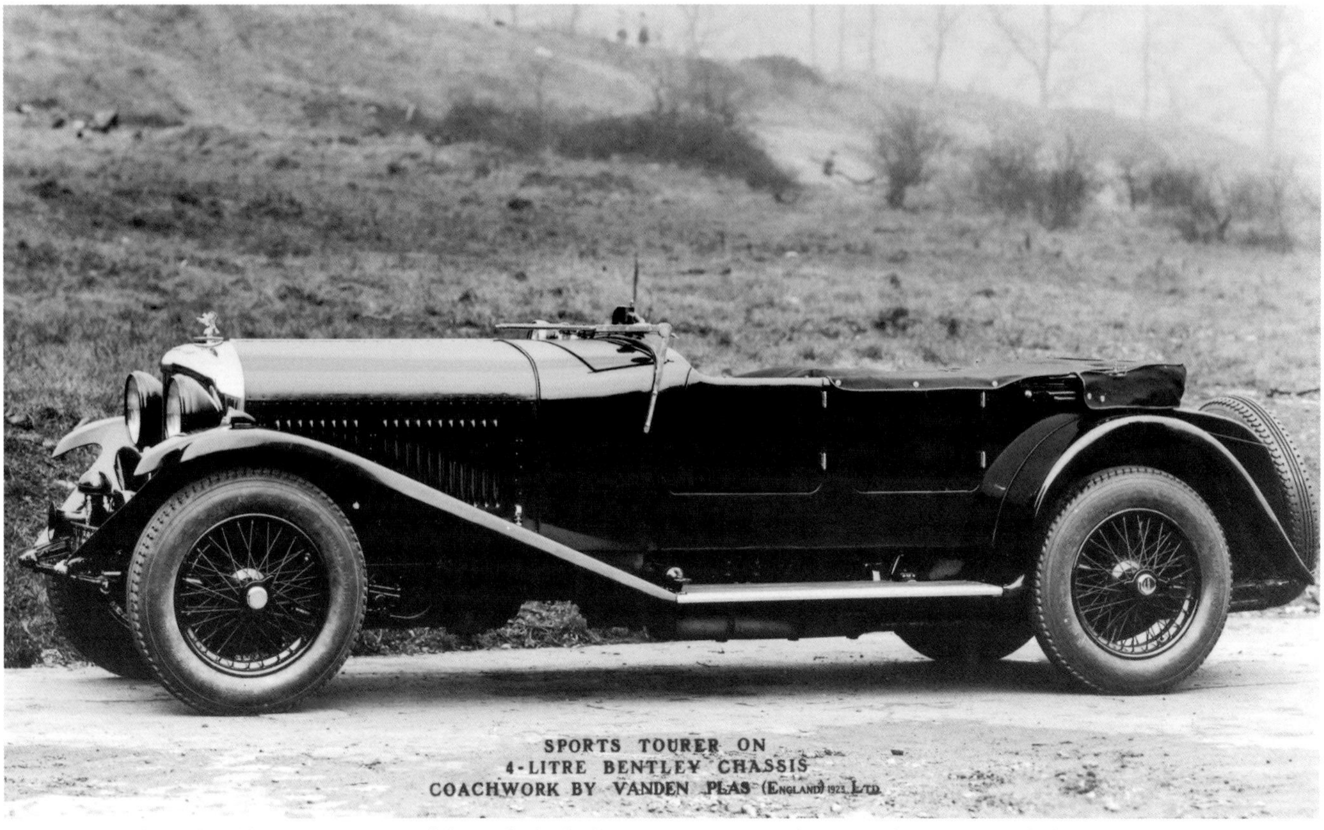

Some chassis from the old company were still being bodied after it had been sold to Rolls-Royce. This Vanden Plas tourer, on Four Litre chassis VA4089, was probably not completed until early 1932.

This attractive Eight Litre Vanden Plas tourer is chassis YX5122. Its construction is of special interest, being described as "silent bloc". This means that it linked sections of the framework with Silentbloc bushes in the manner later to become known as "Silent Travel".

Even later – May 1932 – was this Vanden Plas tourer on Eight Litre chassis YX5111. Here we see the beginnings of the 1930s-style long, low tourer, with a much more subtle front wing line blending into the running-board. The lower overall height is of course helped by the "dropped" chassis of the Eight Litre.

Index